The Book of the Foundation of St. Bartholomew's Church in London.

Early English Text Society.
Original Series, No. 163.

Or Asmoche that the meritory and notable operacions of famose goode and devoute faders yn god sholde be remembred for instruction of after-tymers to theyr consolacion and encres of devocion thys Abbreuyat Tretesse shal compendiously expresse and declare the wonderful and of celestial counsel gracious fundacion of oure hooly placys callyd the Priory of Seynt Barthol' yn Smythfyeld and of the Hospital by olde tyme longyng to the same with other notabilitees expedientli to be knowyn And most specially the glorious and excellent myraclys wroughte with yn them by the Intercessions suffragys and merytis of the forsayd benygne feythfull and blessyd of god Apostyll Saint Bartholomy yn to the laude of almyghty god and acuyacion of his infinite pobere.

ffyrst shal be shewyd who was ffunder of othere hooly placys And howth by grace he was ffyrst Prior of othyr Priory and by howth longe tyme that he contynued yn hys churche yn the honoure the same of most blessyd Bartholomews Apostle fundyd Xayer of goode remembraunce and therin to serue god after the reule of the moost holy fader Austyn agreyest to trewe religiouse men and to thym was pleuse yyy wee vsynge the office and dignite of a Priore Not havynge envnynge of liberal facuce but that that is more emynente than all envnynge ffor he was richd yn purete of consciences Aveuste god by devoyon Aveuste his brethryn by humylite. Aveuste his enemyes with a benyuolence And thus hym self he excercised them pacientli sufferynge of those prowyd purete of soule hryghth maners with honeste probyte expresse deliuraunce yn dyuyne puire.

THE BOOK OF THE FOUNDATION OF ST. BARTHOLOMEW'S CHURCH.
COTTON MS. VESPASIAN B. IX, FOL. 41 R.

The Book of the Foundation of St. Bartholomew's Church in London,

THE CHURCH BELONGING TO THE PRIORY
OF THE SAME IN WEST SMITHFIELD.

EDITED FROM THE ORIGINAL MANUSCRIPT IN THE
BRITISH MUSEUM,
Cotton Vespasian B ix.

BY

SIR NORMAN MOORE, Bart., M.D.,

FELLOW OF THE ROYAL COLLEGE OF PHYSICIANS, CONSULTING PHYSICIAN
TO ST. BARTHOLOMEW'S HOSPITAL, HONORARY FELLOW OF
ST. CATHARINE'S COLLEGE, CAMBRIDGE.

OXFORD

UNIVERSITY PRESS

Great Clarendon Street, Oxford OX2 6DP
United Kingdom

Oxford University Press is a department of the University of Oxford.
It furthers the University's objective of excellence in research, scholarship,
and education by publishing worldwide. Oxford is a registered trade mark of
Oxford University Press in the UK and in certain other countries

© The Early English Text Society 1923

The moral rights of the authors have been asserted

Database right Oxford University Press (maker)

First Edition published in 1923

All rights reserved. No part of this publication may be reproduced,
stored in a retrieval system, or transmitted, in any form or by any means,
without the prior permission in writing of Oxford University Press,
or as expressly permitted by law, or under terms agreed with the appropriate
reprographics rights organization. Enquiries concerning reproduction
outside the scope of the above should be sent to the Rights Department,
Oxford University Press, at the address above

You must not circulate this book in any other form
and you must impose this same condition on any acquirer

Published in the United States of America by Oxford University Press
198 Madison Avenue, New York, NY 10016, United States of America

British Library Cataloguing in Publication Data
Data available

Library of Congress Cataloging in Publication Data
Data available

Original Series, 163

ISBN 978-0-85-991901-2

1123-1923.

TO THE MEMORY OF

Rahere,

FOUNDER OF ST. BARTHOLOMEW'S CHURCH AND HOSPITAL

IN SMITHFIELD, LONDON,

THIS, THE OLDEST RECORD IN ENGLISH,

SETTING FORTH THE STORY OF HIS BENEFICENT PIETY,

IS REVERENTLY DEDICATED

by the Early English Text Society

ON THE OCCASION OF

THE EIGHT HUNDREDTH ANNIVERSARY

OF THE FOUNDATION.

CONSOLABITUR ERGO DOMINUS SION, ET CONSOLABITUR OMNES RUINAS EIUS: ET PONAT DESERTUM EIUS QUASI DELICIAS, ET SOLITUDINEM EIUS QUASI HORTUM DOMINI.

Isaiah li. 2.

ON RAHERE'S TOMB.

PREFATORY NOTE.

THE eight hundredth anniversary of the foundation of St. Bartholomew's Hospital will, alas, be held without the gracious presence of one whose loving zeal and devotion to the Hospital, its history, and all its traditions, will for ever be associated therewith. Over five and thirty years ago Sir Norman Moore had taken in hand the preparation of the present text. For some reason, the work, though far advanced, remained at a stand-still. About a year ago Sir Norman seemed gratified at my suggestion that, in view of the forthcoming Commemoration, the publication of this text, so long delayed, would be a fitting tribute to the memory of the Founder as well as to the beneficent work of the Hospital. He promised to do his part, expressing the hope that it might be possible to add the original Latin. This he was not fated to carry through. The Preface has been left as written by him in 1885. Miss M. M. Weale has revised the text, recollated it with the manuscript, and added the Glossary.

In dedicating this edition of the Book of the Foundation to the name and fame of Rahere, we would fain pay due tribute to the revered memory of the lamented editor, the physician and historian of St. Bartholomew's Hospital, whose loss is so deeply deplored.

I. G.

March 1, 1923.

THE BOOK OF THE FOUNDATION OF ST. BARTHOLOMEW'S.

ALL the accounts of the foundation of St. Bartholomew's Hospital and of the Priory of St. Bartholomew which have hitherto been published, with almost everything which has been written about the founder, are based directly or indirectly upon a manuscript called *Liber fundacionis ecclesie Sancti Bartholomei Londoniarum pertinentis prioratui eiusdem in Weste Smythfelde.* The manuscript measures $10\frac{1}{4}$ in. by $7\frac{1}{8}$ in., and is written on vellum, containing eighty-six leaves of vellum, and encased in a modern binding. It is preserved in the British Museum, and is numbered "Vespasian B IX." This title is taken from the bust which surmounted the book-case which contained the manuscript in the Cottonian collection. It was a fortunate chance for us that the book stood beneath the tenth Cæsar, for the fire which in 1731 destroyed a part of that splendid collection began at the opposite end of the room, and injured many of the contents of the cases surmounted by the earlier emperors. With the Cottonian collection the manuscripts came to the British Museum. Records of four of its former owners are to be found on its leaves. On the first page is written, "Thomas Cotton." He was son of Sir Robert Cotton, who died 1631, and was no doubt the last of the private owners of the manuscript whose names are recorded on its pages. On a vacant page at the end an earlier owner has written, "*Iste liber pertinet ad Thoma*m *Otwell de London;*"[1] and below the title is the autograph of a

---

[1] Lower down on the same page is written "Tomas Powell of London, stacioner;" also—
    (1) Si spie tunc sporte si non spie tunc steale in deade.
    (2) What shall the maisters do at last
        When ser*ua*unts bribe and steale so ffast
    (3) la dama mitrasse il guanto di mano
        ed io l'annello di dito a lei.
and on leaf 78 b, which is otherwise blank, "Mistres Otwell, I bid you farewell, for you do exell and in bewtie heareth the Bell," and "Quis est iste Rex glorie."

third owner, probably intermediate between Otwell and Cotton, "Ri. St. George Norroy King of Arms." Sir Richard St. George was Norroy King at Arms from 1603 to 1623. On the same page as his name, and continuous with the title, is the record of the original ownership of the manuscript, "pertinent*is* prioratui eiusdem in Weste smythfelde." This, with the title, is in the same character as the MS. itself, while the other entries are in several modern hands. It proves that the manuscript belonged to the Priory of St. Bartholomew in Smithfield. When that foundation was broken up at the general dissolution of the monasteries, this book left the library of the Augustinian canons, and was turned out into the world like its masters. A careful search in the libraries descended from those formed in London in the sixteenth century will probably discover some of its shelf companions, but at present it is the only surviving relic of the library[1] of the priory. The manuscript contains two versions of the same work; the first, of forty leaves, in Latin; the second, of thirty-eight leaves, in English. The Latin is in a straight Gothic character with large letters: the English is in a less vertical and differently shaped: a manuscript, of about the year 1400, in the Cambridge University Library, exhibits, as Mr. Henry Bradshaw pointed out to me, a similar distinction between the character in which Latin and that in which English is written. There is no colophon stating the name of the composer or of the scribe, or the date of the composition, or of the writing, but there is internal evidence which makes it possible to determine both. The author states that he belonged to the Priory of St. Bartholomew, and to the Augustinian Order. He was one of the thirty-five canons who formed the community in his time. Many details throughout the work confirm the truth of this statement, while his use without special note of quotation of the words of a charter of Henry I., which was the most precious muniment of the priory, is strong confirmatory

---

[1] In a deed which, by the kindness of the Dean and Chapter, I have examined at St. Paul's, three other volumes of this library are mentioned—a psalter and gloss in two volumes, and the Epistles of St. Paul. The deed, of which some parts are a little faded, is of the year 1250, and states that Richard of Wendover gave these books to the Prior and Convent of St. Bartholomew, and that they received him into their fraternity. The Antiphonarium, mentioned in Rahere's life, makes a fourth volume of this library. A finely-illuminated MS. in the British Museum, said to belong to the Priory, contains evidence that it was the property of the hospital, which had a library of its own.

evidence. Several statements of the author show that he was living, and probably wrote, in the latter part of the reign of King Henry II. He mentions no later king. He says that he had talked with those who remembered Rahere, who died September 20, 1143, and that he himself had been a canon during the priorate of Thomas, Rahere's successor, who died January 18, 1174. He speaks of ecclesiastical privileges obtained from several popes, from Anastasius IV., who reigned 1153—1154, from Adrian IV. (1154—1159), and from Alexander III., Adrian's successor, who died August 30, 1181. Evidence exists that later popes also favoured the priory, and these would certainly have been mentioned had the writer lived to hear of their grants.

More general evidence is his mention of the castle of Munfyches in the city as still standing, for it is known to have been finally demolished in the reign of Henry III. These circumstance, demonstrate the place, the time, and the author of the work. It was composed in the Priory of St. Bartholomew in West Smithfield between the death of Prior Thomas and that of King Henry II., that is, between the years 1174 and 1189, and its author was an Augustinian canon of the Priory. He wore a white rochet with a great black cloak and hood like those upon the effigy on Rahere's tomb, and he kept the canonical hours in the beautiful Norman church, which is all that is now left of his beloved Priory. He was as familiar with our hospital as we are, and the first reports of cases admitted into it are contained in his pages. Adwyne was the name of the first of these reported patients, and he seems to have suffered from long-continued muscular debility, such as is sometimes seen in patients after a long-continued acute illness. The canon wrote in Latin, in a good twelfth-century style. He had read but little of the poets, but had St. Jerome's version of the Bible at his finger ends. He uses its phrases on every possible occasion, and seems as much at home in the Minor Prophets as in the Psalms.

It is only the Latin life which can have been composed in the reign of Henry II. The English version, which contains a few amplifications, is proved by its language to be of later date; and since the existing Latin manuscript and the English were clearly written on parchment at the same period, the date of the English version fixes that of the manuscript as it stands. The language is Middle English, and the character that of about the year 1400.

The scribe has supplied by a slip of his pen an important indication of his period. In the middle of the translation where the original Latin has "Henry II.," he has given "Richard II." as the king's name. The Latin version was written before any Richard had reigned in England, and nothing is more likely than that a scribe, who had lived with Richard II. on the throne, should inadvertently put the name of the reigning king for that of a past sovereign of the same number but of a different name.

To sum up the facts: the manuscript in the British Museum was written about the year 1400, and the English translation was composed at that period. The Latin manuscript, also transcribed then and rubricated in the same style, was originally composed about the year 1180.

Besides its interest to us in St. Bartholomew's, the manuscript well deserves a careful perusal for the glimpses which it gives of life in London in the reign of Henry II. Space compels me to leave it to speak for itself, only adding that the reader must bear in mind that the Augustinian canon's object was to write the spiritual history of our founder and his foundation, and not to compose a detailed historical work. This life of Rahere is now published in full for the first time. I have chosen the English version because it has an interest as an example of our prose literature soon after the time of Chaucer. In the text I have expanded the contractions, which are very few and so often repeated as to present no difficulties; and I have otherwise printed the words exactly as they are in the manuscript, adding a few notes solely with a view to making the perusal easy to a general reader. There are very few words which are not easily intelligible when sound and not spelling is regarded. The precise evidence as to the date of the foundation of St. Bartholomew's Hospital given in the manuscript, and many other facts elucidated by it deserve consideration, but would add too much to the length of this introduction. I hope on a future occasion to set forth in detail the whole life of our Founder.

NORMAN MOORE.

September 20, 1885.

[LIBER I.¹]

(Cotton MS., Vespasian B ix.)

* FOR Asmooche / that the meritory and notable operacyons / of famose / goode ; and deuoute faders yn God / sholde be remembred for Instruccion of aftyr cummers, to theyr consolacioun / and encres of deuocion / thys Abbreuyat Tretesse / shal
5 compendiously expresse and declare / the wondreful, and of celestial concel, gracious fundacion / of oure hoely placys callyd the Priory of seynt Bartholomew yn Smythfyld, and of the hospital by olde tyme longyng to the same / with other notabiliteis expediently to be knowyne. And most specially / the gloriouse and excellent
10 myraclys wroghte with-yn them / by the Intercessions, suffragys, and meritys of the forsayd / benygne, feythfull, and blessid of God Apostyl, Sanctᵗ Bartholomy / yn-to the laude of almyghty God, and agnicioun of his infinite powere.

* [f. 41]

¶ **Fyrst shal be shewyd who was Funder of owere hoely places / and howh, by grace / he was Fyrst pryor of owre priory / and by howh longe tyme that he contynued yn the same.**

Thys chirche, yn the honoure of most blessid Bartholomew
15 Apostle / fundid / Rayer / of goode remembraunce / and theryn to serue God / aftir the rewle of the moost holy fader Austyn / aggregat to-gidire religiouse men / and to them was prelate .xxii. yere / vsynge the office and dignite of a Priore / Not hauynge cunnynge of liberal science, / but / that / that is more emynente
20 than all cunnynge. For he was richid yn puryte of conscience
¶ Ayenste ² god by deuocyoun / Ayenste his brethryne by humylite.

---
¹ The MS. begins as above, without any heading of Book or Chapter, and the first sixteen lines form a sort of preface which is not in the Latin. Then follows in red the title of the first chapter, and then the text begins with a large and beautifully illuminated T. The heading of each subsequent chapter is in red, with a red number in the margin.
² towards (erga).

FOUNDATION

Ayenste his enemyes with a benyuolence. And thus hym-self he
excercised them, paciently sufferynge / Whoose prouyd puryte of
soule / bryght maners, with honeste probyte / experte diligence yn
dyuyne se*r*uyce / *prudent besynes¹ yn temperalle mynystracyun /
in hym were gretly to prayse and co*m*mendable / In festis he was 5
sobir / and namely the folowere of hospitalite / tribulacio*u*ns of
wrecchis / and necessiteys of the pouer' peple oportunyly ad-
myttyng / paciently supportyng, competently spendynge.² In
prosperite nat ynpridid. In adue*r*site paciente / And what-su*m*-
euere / vnfortune / ranne ageyne hym / he restyd hymself vndir' 10
the schadowe of his patrou*n* / that he worshippid³ / whom he
clippid to hym / with-yn the bowell of his soule. In whose helpe,
for all perelles he was sekyr and p*r*eseruyd. Thus he, subiett to
the kyng of blisse : with alle mekenesse / preuydyd with alle
diligence / that were necessarie to his subiectys⁴ / And so prouyd- 15
ynge, he encresid dayly / to hymself, before God and man*e* grace /
to the place reuerence / to his frend*is* gladnesse / to his enemyes
peyne / to his aftircu*m*mers ioye. And suche, certeyn, was the
lyef of hym, aftir his conue*r*syou*n*, bettyr than hit was beforn*e* / In
goodnes eue*r*more encresid. And yn what ordir' he sette the 20
fundament of this temple. yn fewe wordys lette vs shewe / as they
testified to vs that sey hym / herd hym / and were presente yn his
werkys and dedis / of the whiche su*m*me haue take ther' slepe yn
cryiste. And su*m*me of them be ȝitte a-lyue / and wytnesseth of
that / that we schall aftir' say. 25

¶ CAP*IT*U*L*UM 2ᵐ.

¶ What lyef / he ledde a-forn*e* his conuersiou*n*.

THys man*e*, sprongyng⁵ or boryn*e* of lowe lynage⁶ / whan he
attayned the floure of yougth / he begane to haunte the
housholdys of noble men and the palic*is* of pryncys / where,
vndir' euery elbowe of them / he sprede her' coshynys⁷ / with iapys
and flateryng*is*, delectably anoyngtyng her' eerys / by this man*er* 30
to drawe to hym ther' frendschippis. And ȝitte he was nat co*n*tent
with this / but ofte hawntid the kyng*is* palice / and amo*n*ge the

---

¹ business (*sollicitudo*).   ² "n" overlined later.   ³ quem venerabatur.
⁴ *subdito gregi*.   ⁵ *oriundus*.   ⁶ *prosapia*.   ⁷ *pulvillos*.

noysefull prese. of that tumultuous courte, inforsid * hymself with   *[f. 42]
iolite and carnale suauyte / by the whiche he myght drawe to hym
the hertys of many oone / ther', yn spectaclis / yn metys¹ / yn
playes² / and othir' courtly mokkys³ and trifyllys intendyng / he lede
forth the besynesse of alle the day.⁴ And nowe to kyng*is* attendens /
now folowyng the entente of grete men / presid yn proferynge seruyce
that myght plece them / besily so occupied hys tyme that he
myghte opteyne the rathir' the peticions that he wolde desire of
them. Thiswyse to kyng and grete men, gentyll and courtyours
y-knowen / famylier' and felowly⁵ he was. This manere of leuynge
he chose yn his begynnyng / and yn this ex*er*cisid his yough: but
the inwarde-seer'⁶ and m*er*cyfull God of all / the whiche oute of
Mary Magdalene. cast oute .vii. feendys / the whiche to the Fysshere
ȝaue þe keyes of heuyn*e* / mercyfully conu*er*tid this man fro the
erroure of hys way / and addid to hym, so conu*er*ted, many ȝiftys
of vertu / for why they that are fonnysch and febill in the worldys
reputacioun / oure Lorde chesith, to / confounde the myghte of the
worlde.

CAPITULUM 3ᵐ·

¶ Here foloweth howe, conu*er*tid, he wente to Rome.

This man therfore, by the grace of God / of his synnes su*m*tyme
penytent, a-p*ur*posyng to halfe⁷ his dayes / that he myghte
obteyne parfite and plener*e* pardou*n* and indulgence of his
synnes; to that entente he decreid yn hym self to go to the courte
of Rome / couetyng yn so grete a laboure to do the worthy fruytes
of penaunce. The whiche habite of heuynly inspirid soule and
purpos, he wolde nat with a slowthfull mynde be deferrid yn-to
tymes and yeres / but the conceyued goode dede, by feithfull desire
constawntly executynge / he toke his way / oure lord God direct-
yng his pace⁸ / and hole and sownde,⁹ whydir he purposid came /
Where, at the martirdomes¹⁰ of the blessid Apostles Petir' and
poule, he, wepynge † hys dedis and reducyng to mynde¹¹ the scapis¹²   †[f. 42 v.]
of his yougth and ignoraunces / prayd to oure lorde for remyssiou*n*
of them, behestynge furthermore. noon like to do / but thyes vtterly

---

¹ banquets (*epulis*).   ² pastimes (*jocis*).   ³ nonsense (*nugis*).
⁴ *tota die intendere negociun ducebat.*   ⁵ socius.   ⁶ inspector.
⁷ dimidiare   ⁸ domino gressus ejus dirigente.   ⁹ incolumis.
¹⁰ places of martyrdom (*martiria*).   ¹¹ ad memoriam reducens.   ¹² delicta.

to forsake / euer deuoutly his will promyttyng to obeye. These .ii.
clere lightys of heuyn, .ii. men of mercy, Petir' and Poule, he
ordeyned mediatoures / betwyne hym and the lorde of all erthe /
promysynge that he wolde be ware / of alle passid vnhabilnesse,[1]
and yeue affectualy his diligence and laboure / to that he hathe 5
promysyd / and whyle he taryed ther / in that meene whyle / he
began to be vexed with greuous sykenesse / and his doloures. litill
and litill takynge ther' encrese / he drewe to the extremyte of lyf /
the whiche dredynge with-yn hymself / that he nat ȝitte for his
synnys hadde satisfied to God / and therfore he supposid that God 10
toke vengeawnce of hym for his synnys a-mongis owte-landisshe
peple / and demyd the last oure of oure of[2] his deith drewe hym nygh.
Thys remembrynge inwardly / he schedde owte as water his herte
in the syght of God / and albrake owte in terys; than he avowyd,
yf helthe God hym wolde grawnte, that he myght lefully returne to 15
his contray[3] / he wolde make an[4] hospitale. yn recreacioun of poure
mene, and to them so there I-gaderid / necessaries mynystir' / aftir
his power' / And nat long aftir' / the benigne and mercyfull lord /
that byhelde þe terys of Eȝechie / the kynge. The importune
prayer of the womane of Chananee / rewardid with the benefeit 20
of his pite / Thus lykewyse mercyfully he behelde this wepyng
mane, and gaf hym his helth / Approuyd his Avowe / so of his
sykenes recoueryd he was, and in short tyme hole y-maade begane
homwarde to come / his vowe to fulfille that he hadde made.

¶ CAPITULUM 4ᵐ·

Of the[5] visioun that he sawe in the way, and of the commaundement of seynt Bartholomew the apostle.

*[f. 43] Whan he wolde parfite his way that he hadde begone * / In 25
a certayne nyght he sawe a visioun full of drede[6] and
of swetnesse / whan, aftir' the labourous and swetyng
that he had by dayes / his body with reste he wolde refresshe. It
semyd hym to be bore vp An hye / of a certeyne beiste hauynge
.iiii. feete and .ii. wynggis: and sette hym yn an hye place; and 30

---

[1] folly (*ineptiis*).   [2] So in MS.   [3] *ad patriam suam sibi redire liceret.*
[4] MS. and.   [5] "the" *twice in MS.*   [6] terrore.

whan he from so grete an highnesse / wolde inflecte and bowe
downe his yie to the lower party¹ donward / he behelde an
horrible pytte / whose horryble beholdyng ynpressid in hym, the
beholder, grete drede and horroure. For the depnesse of the same
5 pytte was depper than eny man myghte atteyne to see. Therfore
he, secrete knowere of his defautes / demyd hym self to slyde in-to
that cruell a-downcast / and therfore, as hym semyd ynwardly. / he
fremyshid,² and for drede tremelyd / and grete cryes of his
moweth procedyd. To wham dredyng and for drede criynge,
10 apperid a certeyn mane pretendynge in chere³ the maieste of a
kynge / of grete bewte / and imperiall auctorite / and his yie one
hym fastnyd / he seyd goode wordes / wordes of consolacioun
bryngynge goode tydyngis, as he schulde sey in this yn this⁴ wyse /
"O mane," he seyd / "What and howe muche seruyce shuldes
15 thou yeue to hym / that yn so grete a perele hath brought helpe
to the / " Anonne he answerde to this seyynge / " whatsumeuer
myght be of hert and of myghtys / diligently shulde .I. yeue, in
recompence to my delyuerer'." And than saide he, " .I. am
Bartholomew, the Apostle of Ihesu crist, þat come to socoure the
20 yn thyne Angwysshe / and to opyne to the. the secrete mysteryes of
heuyn / knowe me trewly / by the will and commaundemente of
the hye Trinite / and the comyne fauoure of the Celestiall Courte
and consell / to haue chosyn) a place yn the Subbarbis of Londone,
at Smythfeld; wher' yn myn name thou shalte founde A Chirche /
25 and it shall be the house of God / ther shalbe the tabernacle of
the * lambe / the temple of the Holy Gost / ¶ This spirituall howse,   f. 43 v.]
almyghty God. shalle ynhabite / and halowe yt / and glorifie yt:
And his yene shall be opyn / and his Eerys yntendyng one this
howse, nyght and day / that the asker yn hit schall resceyue / the
30 seker' shall fynde / and the rynger' or knokker' shall entre.
¶ Trewely euery soule conuertid / penytent of his synne / And in
this place prayng / yn heuyn) graciously schall be herde. The
seekere with parfite herte / for whatsumeuyr tribulacioun, with
owte dowte / he schalle fynde helpe / To them that with feithfull
35 desire knoke At the doyr of the Spowse / assistent Angelys shalle
opyne the gatis of heuyn / receyuyng and offeryng to God the
prayers and vowys of feithfull peple. ¶ Wherfore thyn handys
be there confortid in God / hauyng in hym truste / do thou

---

¹ ad ima.   ² shuddered (inhorruit).   ³ mien (vultu).   ⁴ So in MS.

manly!¹ Nethir of the costis of this bildynge dowte the nowght / onely yeue thy diligence / and my parte schalbe to prouyde necessaries / directe / bilde / & ende this werke / and this place / to me accepte / with euydent tokenys and signys protecte and defende contynually hyt / vndyr the schadowe of my wyngys / and therfore of this werke knowe me the maister / ¶ And thy self onely the mynyster / Vse diligently thy seruyce / and .I. shall schewe my lordeschippe." In these wordes the visioun disparyschydde.²

¶ **CAPITULUM 5ᵐ·**

¶ **What he yn hymself tretid of thys visyn).**

HE, awakid, begane to reuolue wysly in his mynde. that he hadde seyne / In that meene while / to his flittyng soule³ was mewyd to haue a dowtable sentence⁴ / whethir it schulde be hadde / and take for a fantastykke illusyoun / that ofte happyth to men / yn ther slepe / or for an heuynly warnyng or Answere / the whiche he demyd himself nat worthy to haue. Thus stryvyd togedyr in his herte / feithfull mekenesse / and drede / and vncertayn he * was / to whom more credence schulde be gowyne. And as a meke mane, he wolde them haue hydde, and nat presume hier thyngis aboue hym self than he vndrestode. Also tymorosely he dred to laches⁵ the preceptis of the Apostle, and so lachesynge⁶ / nat meke / but prowte / to be bownde / with the streite examinacion of the hie Iuge. Therfore, with worthier sentences and better allegacion whan he was informyd / drede of God and the Apostle optenyd the victorye / to whom grace was felowschippe. and blessedly areysid vp the meke man / confortid the faynt-hertid / the suatperynge mane⁷ / stedfastid / The goode forseyd dede, in stabill degre, with his welsumme and happy purpose to parfourme. He therfore, techynge hym inwardly / as we beleue / by his vnccioun, that beforne hadde instructe hym by nyghtly vision, ordaynyd / to make parfite that was commawnded / namely, whyle he was commawnded oonly and grettely to yeue diligence and laboure. And soethly the ouerplues shulde be as

---

¹ viriliter age.   ² disparuit.   ³ fluctuanti animo.   ⁴ dubiam sentenciam.
⁵ to disregard (negligere).   ⁶ negligendo.   ⁷ initantem.

the commawnder wolde ordeyne. Trewly by dremys many secretis of Goddis wille / hath come to the knowleche of men / In the seryous[1] scripture / of the olde / and newe testamentis / as nat onys but oftyn we haue redde / wherof oone wittnesse / of them bothe / sufficith vs. to bryngforth. ¶ Holy Danyel in his dreme lernyd the dreme of the kynge /. and the interpretacioun of the same / oure Lorde reuelynge, he knewe / Rightwus Ioseph, yn his slepe / was warnyd nat to drede to take Marye his Wyf / And, stondynge the Article of parsecucioun / to flee with her in-to Egipte. And whan herode, the autoure of parsecucion, was deed / by the Angle he was commaunded to returne aȝen in-to Iurye. ¶ Visions in nyght tymes I-made / pretende nat alway. cause of deseit / but sumtyme pregnant & frutefull sentences of heuenly mystery / worthy to be trowid / with feith and admiracion. *With theys / and many moo auctorites of scripture / we ben taght; of the whiche to haue parfite discrecion .I. trowe[2] y[s][3] nat / of mannys witte / but of a godly gyfte. And therfore after the lawe, the residue of the lambe, lat vs leue yt to the fyre, that ys, the hoely gooste.[4]

* [f. 44 v.]

¶ CAPITULUM 6ᵐ.

¶ Exposicion of this vision.

FOrthermore, what yf it be / inquerid what pretendith the vision of the federyd beiste / what the horrible pitte / what settyng of the man an hye / what .I. -feill of this / in fewe wordis I schalle expresse. I deme / the beiste to signifie the deuyl, the whiche in Eȝechiel mysterially / ys callid the grete egle. / Nowe for the dignite of heuenly nature / Nowe for magnitude of spirituall wykkednes / the whiche, bothe there yn Eȝechiel / and also in this vision / the beyste semyd grete wyngis to haue // by that ys vnderstonde, he, swollyn with pride of elacion, proposid in will to be like almyghty God / and to the same elacyon, man with deceyuable promysse proudly he arysyd[5] aȝenste his creator / with the whyche synne neuer cesith he / to attaste[6] alle

---

[1] serie.   [2] think (reor).   [3] MS. yt.
[4] Chapter V. in the Latin ends with the words "ideo secundum legem: relinquamus igni," so that the translator has here added a gloss of his own.
[5] superbe erexerit.   [6] attemptare.

the kynde of men / many to ynfoldeyn / and many with hym to
adde / to euerlastyng fyre / no houre ne tyme cessith not / Hys
.iiij. feete ben .iiii. wyndys, of the whiche is spoken yn Zacharie /
Or els .iiii. gendrys of temptacioun / the whiche anumbrith the
psalnyst; or els .iiii. vices, of the whiche spekith the prophete
Ioel, seiyng : " The residue of the Eruce etyth the buttyrflye / and
the residue of the buttyrflie etyth brucus / and the residue of bruce
etythe rubigo " / vndirstondyng lecherie by Eruca / by the buttyrflie, Vaynglorie / by brucus, glutteny / by rubygo, Ire signifiyng,
and wrath / ¶ Note well that Eruca ys a worme [1] / that / growith
of the worttys / Locusta that fleith frome floure to floure / brucus
is the Issue / of the buttyrflie / or he haue wyngis.   ¶ Of .iiii.
wyndys, remembrith Zacharie [2] seiynge,* " I lyfte vp my eiyn and
sawhe / and to me was seyed, ' beholde .iiii. hornnys ' / And .I.
seied to the Angle. that spake in me / ' what ben theys ? ' And he
seide to me / ' these ben the hornnys / that shall blowe and ventilatte.[3] Iude / Israel / and Ierusalem.' " By þe which .iiii. wyndys
be signified / .iiii. passions of þe soule, that ys to seye / drede /
and heuynesse / Loue and gladnesse [4] / that dissipate alweyes the
quyete of mynde / and no soule ther / is bownde with bridyll,
where theys regne.   ¶ Of .iiii. gendres of temptacioun, seide Dauid
of the rightwes mane / thus [5] / " Thou schalt nat drede for the
nyghte / drede / ne for the Arrow fleynge in the day / ne for the
besynes [6] Walkynge in derknesse / ne for the yncourse [7] and
mydday devyl." // The fyrste temptacioun is lighte and hydde /
the secunde lighte and opyne / the thirdde greuous and hydde /
the .iiii[th.] greuous and opyne ¶ With these And beforseyd maners,
as be his feete / this synguler ennemy of mankynde compressith vs
to the erthe. And so to hym he throwythe dowyn) men, And
them so prostrate, with horrible cleys of malice violently con-

---

[1] That which the palmer worm hath left hath the locust eaten: and that which the locust hath left hath the cankerworm eaten, and that which the cankerworm hath left hath the caterpillar eaten.—Joel i. 4. The sentence beginning *Note well*, is an addition of the translator.

[2] Then I lifted up mine eyes, and saw, and behold four horns. And I said unto the angel that talked with me, What be these? And he answered me, These are the horns which have scattered Judah, Israel, and Jerusalem.— Zech. i. 18, 19.   [3] ventilaverunt.

[4] Timor et tristicia,
    Amor et leticia.

[5] Thou shalt not be afraid for the terror by night; nor for the arrow that flieth by day; nor for the pestilence that walketh in darkness; nor for the destruction that wasteth at noonday.—Psalm xci.

[6] *besynes* represents the *negocio* of the Vulgate.   [7] *incursu*.

strayneth. And furthermore, mene adherent wilfully to hym /
he drawith from vice in-to vice / from Evillis to wors / compelleth
them to breke owte of rewle / tyl his synnys bene complete, and
as he were lyfte vp / yn-to the hye towre of all wikkidnesse / where
5 God vengynge / they falle downe / in-to the lowest of the pytte,
that ys, into þe mooste profunde helle / ordeyned for wrecchis,
and of all wrecchis moost wrecchidde.

¶ By this vision I trowe be signified to mane / that he shulde
attende / And considre / the manyfolde snarys / of oure sotell
10 ennemy prudently / And aware them holsumly[1] / leyste that, by
a cruell downecastyng I-suppid vp,[2] wrecchidly he shulde perysche.
¶ But sithen it is not yn mannys wytte, his way / nothir' in his
kunnynge to directe his iornay / there ys * addid to hym consolacioun   * [f. 45 v.]
of heuynly mercy / and nat a litill, but mochyll occasion to optene
15 vertu. And by that moere spedily to deserue godly helpe / by
the whyche besily . he myght fulfille the commawndemente of the
Apostle // I esteme hym a wysman that canne vndirstande by theys
thyngis that Arne shewid to hym / & not I-hidde from hym / but
schewed yn dede and worde what ys to be doyn).

CAPITULUM 7ᵐ·

¶ Howe the kyngès fauore y-hadde . the precepte and his vowe he fulfillid.

20 THerfore .I-passid that remaynyd of his way / he came to
Londone / and of his knowleche[3] / and frendis with grete
ioye was receyued / with whiche also with the Barons of
Londone he spake famylyary / of these thynges / that were turnyd
and sterid in his herte / And of that was done Abowt hym / in the
25 way, he tellid it owte. And what schulde ben done of this / he
cowncellid // ¶ Of them toke he this Answere / that noone of
these myght be parfityd / but the kynge were firste I-cowncellid -
Namely, sith the place godly[4] to hym y-schewid. was conteyned
withyn the kyngis market / of the whyche it was not leuefull to
30 prynces or other lordys, of there propyr' auctoritate eny thyng to
mynnysse / nethyr ʒitte to so solempne an obsequy depute / Ther-

---

[1] salubriter caveret.   [2] absortus.   [3] a notis.   divinitus.

fore, vsyng theys mennys cowncell, In oportune tyme he dressed
hym / to the kynge / and before hym—and the Bisshoppe Richarde[1]
beynge presente / the whiche he hadde made to hym fauorable
byforne /—effectually expressid his besynes, and that he myght
leuefully / brynge his purpose to effecte / mekely besought / And
nyh hym was he / in whoes hande it was / to what he wolle / the
kyngis herte ynclyne ; And yneffectualle these prayers myght nat
be / whoes auctor ys the Apostle / whois gracyous herer[2] was God /
his worde, therfore, was plesaunte / and acceptable in the kyngis
yie / And whane he hadde peysyd[3] the goode wille of the mane
* prudently / as he was wytty[4] / grauntid to the peticioner his kyngly
fauore / benyngly yeuynge auctorite to execute his purpos. And he,
hauynge the title of desirid possessioun of the kyngis maieste, was
right gladde. Than, nothynge he omyttynge of cure and diligence
.ii. werkys of pyte begane to make. Oone for the vowe / that he
hadde made / An othyr' as to hym by precepte was inioynyde.
Therfore as the case prosperously succedid / And aftyr the Apostles
word, all necessaryes flowid vnto the hande / the Chirche he
made of cumly stoonewerke tabylwyse. And an hospitall howse
a.litill lenger' of / from the chirche by hymself / he began to
edifie.

¶ The Chirche was fowndid / as we haue take of oure eldres, In
the moneth of Marche, In the name of oure lorde Ihesu crist / in
memorie of mooste blesside Bartholomewe Apostle / the yere from
the Incarnacioun of the same lorde oure sauyoure .M$^{mo.}$C$^{mo.}$xxiii. /
thanne haldyng and rewlyng the holy see of Rome, mooste holy
fadir Pope Calixte[5] the secunde / presidente in the chirche of
Inglond / William,[6] Archebisshoppe of Cawntirbury ; And Richarde,[7]
Bysshoppe of Londone, the whiche, of due lawe and right, halowid
that place yn the Eiste party of the forsayde felde, and bysshoply
auctoryte dedicate the same / that tyme fulbreue and shorte[8] as a
cymytory. Regnyng, the yonger son / of William Nothy / first

[f. 46]

---

[1] *Richard de Belmeis*, elected Bishop of London May 24, 1108 ; died Jan. 16, 1128.
[2] exauditor. [3] perpendens. [4] prudenti ut erat pectori.
[5] Calixtus II., elected February 1, 1119 ; died December 12, 1124.
[6] William de Curbuil, elected archbishop February 4, 1123 ; died November 26, 1136.
[7] Richard de Belmeis, elected May 24, 1108 ; died January 16, 1128 ; but he was disabled from public affairs by an attack of hemiplegia in the latter half of 1123.
[8] breve tunc admodum cimiterium.

kynge of Englischemen / yn the North, Herry the firste¹ xxx^{ty.} yere / And a-sidehalfe the thirde yere of his reigne ; to the laude And glorie of the hye and indyuyduall Trynyte : to hym, blessynge, thankynge, honoure, and Empyer', worlde with-owtyne ende!
5 Amen!

CAPITULUM 8^{m.}

¶ What was yn reuelacyon shewyd to kynge Edwarde of this place.

HEir' we may nat silence kepe, but euydently expresse, that by relacioun of oure senyoures, we* haue fownde, dyuynly schewid / this to be a place of prayer / longe beforne tyme / to the glorious kynge Edwarde the confessoure / the son of
10 Etheldrede the kynge, brothir' of seynt Edwarde the martir / of whome many goode thyngis, they seye, they hadde herde in ther tymes, nowe to be declarid. ¶ Thys blessid kyng, whan he was in the Chirche of God / replete with manyfolde bewte of vertu / as the boke of his Gestys declarith / as a religious and full of the
15 spirite of prophicie, he schoone bright / beholdyng thynges fer of² / as they were presente. And thynges to cumme, as they were nowe existente / with the yis of his soule / by the holy goste for he was Illumyned. ¶ The whiche, in a certayne nyght whan he was bodely slepyng, his herte to God wakyng / he was warnyd of thys
20 place with an heuynly dreme made to hym, that Gode this place hadde chosyne / his name ther-yn to be putte and sette / And holy and worschipfull it schulde be schewyd to cristyne peple. Wher-vpone this holy kynge, erly arisyng, come to this place that God hadde shewid hym / And to them that abowte hym stoid / expressid
25 the vision, that nyght made to hym / seyde before all the peple,

* [f. 46 v.]

---

¹ The Latin MS. reads: "Regnante juniore filio willi nothi primi regis anglorum ex aquilonaribus henrico primo anno xxx.mo et circiter tercium regui ejus ad laudem et gloriam." Henry I. was crowned August 5, 1100, so that the thirty-third year of his reign was from August 5, 1132, to August 4, 1133. The twenty-third year of his reign extended from August 5, 1122, to August 4, 1123. The dates of the ecclesiastics named are : Pope Calixtus, 1119-1124 ; Archbishop William, 1123-1136 ; Bishop Richard, 1108-1128. They prove that the xxx. of the translation and of the Latin are errors of transcription for xx. An important charter was granted to the Priory in 1133, and with this in his mind the scribe might the more easily err. The MS. has Herry.
² far off.

prophecied this place to be gret before God / whoes cleyr prophecyes / howh they be supportyd grettly with the myghte of treweth, experience hath approuyd yt / And euery feithfulmane may cleirly beholde the same.

CAPITULUM 9m.

¶ What .iii. men of greyce seyed beforne of thys place.

IT was seyed that .iii. men of greyke, y-sprongyne of noble lynage, Goynge owte frome ther countre and kynrede / takyng one them for God / the holy laboure of pilgirmage / and whane with deuoute soule they sowght the helpe of seyntis in many places, frome the grete see / they hadde enteryd Inglande / desiryng to visite the bodies of seyntis theyre * restynge / and by ther merytis in the laste examinacioun to be succurrid and defendid / whane they camme to londone / they wente to thys place / and ther, prostrate, honoured and worschippid God / and aforne them / that ther was presente / and behelde them / as symple ydiottys¹ / they begane wondirfuH thyngis to seye / and prophecye of this place, seyynge / "Wondir nat ʒe / vs here to worschippe God / where a fulle acceptable temple to hym / shaH be bylid / For the high maker of aH thyng wyH that it be bylded ; and the fame of this place schaH attayne frome the spryng of the sunne to the goynge downe."

*[f. 47]

5

10

15

20

CAPITULUM 10m.

¶ Of the clensynge of thys place.

TRuly thys place aforne his clensynge / pretendid noone hope of goodnesse / right vncleene it was / and as a maryce dunge and fenny with water almost euerytyme habowndynge / And that / that was emynente, a-boue the water drye / was deputid and ordeyned to the Iubeit or galowys of thevys / and to the tormente of othir that were dampnyd by Iudicialle auctoryte.
¶ Truly whane Rayer hadde applied his study to the purgacioun of this place / and decreid to put his hande to that holy bilyng / he

25

---

¹ tanquam simplices et idiotas.

was nat ignoraunte of Sathanas wyles / for he made and feyned
hym-self vnwyse / for he was so coactid¹ / and owtward pretendid
the cheyr' of an ydiotte / and begane a litiłł while / to hyde the secret-
nesse of his soule / And the moore secretely he wroght / the moore
5 wysely he dyd his werke. ¶ Truly yn playnge wise / and maner /
he drewe to hym the felischipe of children and seruantis / assemblynge hym-self as one of them / and with ther vse and helpe.
stonys and othir thyngis profitable to the bylynge / lightly he
gaderyd to-gedyr / he played with them, and from day to day made
10 hym-self moore vile in his owne* yen / in so mykiłł that he plesid   * [f. 47 v.]
the Apostle of cryiste, to whome he hadde prouyd hym-self.
¶ Thorowgh whois grace and helpe, whan ałł thynge was redy that
semyd necessarie, he reysid vppe a grete frame. And nowe he
was provyd nat vnwyse / As he was trowid / but verry wyse:
15 And that / that was hydde and secrete, opynly begane to be made
to ałł men. ¶ Thus yn merveles wyse, he, comforttid in the holy
gooste / and instructe with cunnynge of trweth / seide the worde
of God feithfully / by dyuerse chirches / And the multitude, bothe
of clerkys / and of the laife² constauntly was exhortid / to folowe
20 and fulfyłł those thynges that were of charite and almesdede.
And yn thys wyse he cumpasid his sermon / that nowe he sterid
his audience to gladnesse / that ałł the peple applaudid him ; And
in-contynent, anoon he proferred sadnesse and sorow of ther synnys /
that ałł the peple were compellid yn-to syghyng and wepyng / but
25 he, trewly yn the same cheir and soule euermore parseueraunte,
expressyd holsumme doctrine / and aftir God / and feithfułł sermon
prechyd. And yn his techynge vnrepreuyd was fownde / those
thyngis techynge / that the holy gost by the Apostles / and
Appostolyke expositoures, haue yeue to the chirche vnmoueably
30 & stedfastly to beholde. Forthermore hys lyfe acorded to his tonge,
and his dede approued wełł hys sermone / and so, yn the sacrifice
of God, the moweth and bylle of the Turtyłł was returnyd to his
Armepittes, and reclyned vnto the wyngys / leisse that he, prechynge
to othir / schulde be fownde reprouable yn hym-self. ¶ Of this
35 almen grettly were astonyd / boeth of the nouelte of the areysid
frame / and of the fownder of this newe werke / Whoe wolde trowe
this place with so sodyan A clensyng to be purgid / and ther' to be
sette vp the * tokenys of crosse !³ And God there to be worshippid /   * [f. 48]

---

¹ *Latin*, coactus.   ² laicorum.   ³ crucis insignia.

where sumtyme stoid the horrible hangynge of thevys / Who shulde nat be astonyid / ther to. se constructe and bylyd, thonorable byldynge of pite. that schulde be a sekir seyntwary. to them / that fledde ther-to / where sumtyme was a comyn officyne[1] of dampnyd peple / and a general / ordeynyd for payne[2] of wrecchys / who schulde nat mervel / þer to be haunttid the mysterie of oure lordys body / and precious blode / where was sumtyme schewid owte the blode of gentyly and hethyn peple! Whois hert lightly schulde take or admytte suche a. man nat producte of gentyl bloode / nat gretly yndewid with litterature of mannys[3] / or of dyuyne kunnynge / so worschipfull, and so grete a worke, prudently to begynne / and hyt begunne, to so happy a progresse / fro day in-to day to perfecte and parforme! ¶ This ys the change of the right hande of God. O cryst, these ben thy workys / that of thyn excellent vertu / and synguler pyte, makyst of vnclene / clene / and chesist the feble of the worlde to confownde the myghty / And callist them / that be nat / as yt wer' they that been / the whiche golgotha, the place of opyne abhominacioun / madist a seyntwary of prayer / and a solempne tokyne or sygne of deuocioun.

CAPITULUM 11ᵐ·

¶ Of the riottys and assemylyngis of the aduersarie partys, and of the pryuylegys of the chirche.

Thus procedynge the tyme / clerkis to leue vndir reguler ynstitucion / In the same place, in breif tyme were vnyd to gidir': ¶ Rayer optenynge cure and office of the priorhede. And mynystrynge to them necessaries, nat of certeyn rentys, but plenteously of oblaciouns of feithfull peple / and nat longe aftyr, that drede that he drade come to hym / And that he dredyd happid hym.* He was to summe the odur' of lyif yn-to lyif / to othir the odur' of deith yn-to deith. Summe seid he was a deseyuer', for cause that yn the nette of the grete Fyscher, evil fischis were medillid[4] with goode / Aforne the houre of the laste disseuerawnce / his howseholde peple were made hys enemyes. And so roys aȝenste hym wyckid men / and wykydnes lyid to hym self.[5]

---

[1] officina.
[2] generalis indicta erat pena.
[3] humanarum literarum.
[4] medillid, admixti.
[5] et insurrexerunt contra eum viri iniqui sed mentita est iniquitas sibi.

therfore with prikkyng enuye, many preuatly / many also opynly / aȝenste the seruant of God cesid nat to gruge / and in derogacioun to the place And prelate of the same, browghtyn many sclawnders with thretnyngis / the goodis that they myght they withdrewe & 5 toke a-wey / constreyned hym. with wykkidnes / made wery hym with iniuries / prouokid hym with despitis / bygilid hym with symulate frendschippis / And summe of them brake owte in to so bolde A wodnesse / that they drewe among them-self A contracte of wikkid conspiracion / what day I-sette and place / the seruant of God 10 they myght, thorowgh wylys and sutilte, draw to ther cowncell wyth a deceyte / and hym so ther present to plukke from the stappis¹ of his lyif. And so his remembraunce they wolde had doyn awey from this worlde. But ther is no wysdom / ther is no kunnyng / ther is no cowncell / ayenste God / In whom he cast 15 his thowght, And with the Apostle put his strengith. ¶ He, therfore, that was his hoope, was his myght / And for hym he discumfyit his ennemyes / therfore whan the day abydde comme / whiche was deputid to the Innocentis deith / oone of them, partner / of so grete a wykkidnesse, secrete to hym self abhorryng so grete 20 a synne, aforyn the houre of this perell drawyng neir' / shewide by ordir to the seruante of God / the summe of / al / ther cowncell / he for this / to God and to his patrone ȝaf thankys / that the *secretes of his ennemyes were nat hýdde fram hym. And that by * [f. 49] the benefete of oure lordes pyte, he hath skapid / the deith to hym 25 arayed² / for thys and lyke causys apperynge. Aȝen he wente to the kyng with a lamentable querell, expressynge howe with vntrew despitys / he was deformyd, And whate fastidious owtbrekyngis hadde temptid hym / besekyng his Royall Munyficence / that his persone And the place that he hadde grauntid hym / he wolde 30 defende. Also yn his suggestion to the kynge, he made. this reson: he bidith no rewarde of God / that hath begunne a goode werke / and so bygunne / with a dew ende / hath nat fynyshid the same / wherfore for the ynward bowellis of the mercy of cryst that he trustid yn / for the dignyte that he schoone with / And for the 35 power of his emynence / he wolde opyn the bosumme of his pite / to them that were desolate / and honoure God yn his seruantes, And restreyn the berkyng wodnesse³ of vnfeithfull peple / so that to the goode bygynnyngis he now ioynyng bettir yssuys, and

¹ steps (vestigio).   ² sibi paratam.   ³ latrantem insaniam.

largeor exsecucions, myghte byle to hym-self eternal howse yn
heuyn, whyle that he worschippith and defendith the howse of
God yn erthe. ¶ Thus the kynge, mervellyng the prudence and
constaunce of this mane, answerd / that he wolde applie hym to
his Iust and nessessarie peticions / And that Furthermore he behestid 5
hym-self to be a tutur and defensur of hym. and of hys / therfore
he made this Chirche with all his pertynenc*is* with the sam
fredo*m*mys that his Crowne ys liberttid with[1] or ony othir chirch
yn all Inglonde / that is most y-freid / and relesid hit all customys
/ and decreid for to be free from*e* all erthly seruyce, power, and 10
subieccio*n* / and ʒaue sharpe sentence aʒenste contrary malyngno*urs*.[2]

[f. 49 v.] This & many othir * Insigniis, that ys to sey dignyteys of liberte /
he gr*a*untid to the pr*i*or / and to them vndirneith hym seruynge,
and to the forsayd Chirche, and with his Chartur and Seel con-
firmyd[3] hyt / adiurynge also all his heyris and successoures. yn 15
name of the holy trinite / that this place w*ith* Royall auctorite /
they vpholde and defende, and the libertees of hym .I.-gr*a*untid /
they schulde graunte and conferme. With suche p*r*iuelegge / thus
whan he was streyngethyd and confortably defendyd / glad he
went owte / from the face of the kynge. And whan he was 20
cu*m*myn home to his / what he had obteynyd of the royall maieste
expressid / to othir / that they schulde ioy with hym. And to
othir that ther schulde be affrayed. Also this worschipfull mane
p*u*rposid for to depose the quarell of his Calamyteys afore the See
of Rome[4] / Goddis grace hym helpynge / and of the same See 25
writynges to brynge / to hym and to his aftyr cu*m*mers profitable /
but dyuerse vndirgrowynge ympedymentys / and, at the last, lettyng
the Article of deith, that he wold had fulfillid / he myght nat.
And so only the reward of good wylle he deseruyd. Aftir his
decese .iii. men . of the same congregacio*u*n, whoys memory be 30
blessid in blisse / sondirly[5] wente to sondirly[5] byschoppis[6]
of the See of Rome / And three p*r*iulegies of three byssshoppys[7]

---

[1] A.D. 1133.   [2] malignantes.
[3] The original of this charter is not extant. It was, however, produced in a court of law by the prior and convent in the reign of Henry VI., and there is in the Hospital a copy made in the same reign. Another copy, not I think the original enrolment, was preserved in the Tower, and is now in the Record Office.
[4] From this it seems probable that the newly-introduced Augustinian canons had their difficulties with the secular clergy. The king had settled all the civil difficulties, the ecclesiastical remained.
[5] singuli singulos.   [6] presules.   [7] pontificum.

obteynyd / that is to seye of seynt*is*[1] Anastace, Adrian, And Alexander / this Chirche witħ three doweryes / as yt were witħ an vnpenytrable scochyn wardid and defendyd aȝenst ympetuous hostylyte. Now beholde, that p*r*ophesye of the blessid kynge and confessoure seynt Edward, that befor*n*e tyme hadde profysyed and seyne by reuelaciou*n* of this place / of grete party is seyn and fulfillid / Beholde trewly, that this holy chirche and chosyn to God, schynetħ* witħ manyfolde bewte ; Fowndyd and endewid witħ heuenly Answer, .I.-sublymate witħ many p*r*iuylegies of notable men, And to a su*m*me of laude And glorie / rychessid witħ many relikys of Seyntes / and bewtyfied w*ith* hawntid[2] and vsuaħ tokenys of celestiaħ vertu. This nat vnprofitably byfore tastid / lette vs draw nere to the narracion of myracles.

*[f. 50]

¶ **CAP*IT*ULUM** 12ᵐ·

¶ **Of ligħt heuenly sent owte.**

15 WHan, therfore, in the forsaid place / at the bygy*n*nyng was made An oratorye. In honoure of the blessid Apostle / many and innume*r*able were schewid tokynnys of myracles / but what for the grete plenty of them / and necligence of writyng of the same / they be almoyste vnremembred / wherfore of these a fewe / specially of these that lattir dayes were knowe to vs more by sigħt / than by heryng / As they cam to oure mynde feitħfully we shaħ teħ. In the begynnynge of this areysed frame / oure senyo*u*res tellid vs / that on*e* a day at evensong tyme / whan derkenys drew vpo*n* / ther was séyn a ligħt from heuyn sent schynynge on*e* this Chirche / Abidynge there vppon*e* / the space of an howre / that they sawe them-self / and many othir men also / the whiche lygħt aftir. returnyd up An hye, & to no man*e* aftirwarde aperid / and that yn a moment was take a-wey from the yis of the beholders. ¶ Howe grete a tokyn*e* this was of pite and grace heuynly / opynly aftirward was schewid / by multitude of toknys yn the same place.

¹ Anastasius IV. reigned July 9, 1153—December 2, 1154. Adrian IV. reigned December 3, 1154—August 30, 1159. Alexander III. reigned September 7, 1159—August 30, 1181.
² frequentissimis. The words of the charter here referred to are "hanc autem ecclesiam cum omnibus que ad eam pertinent sciatis me velle manutenere et defendere et liberam esse sicut coronam meam et accepisse in manu mea et in defensione contra omnes homines."

¶ CAPITULUM 13ᵐ·

¶ Of Wolmer contract and there .I.-curid.

There was . an sykeman, Wolmer be name, with greuous and longe langoure depressid / and wrecchid to Almen / that hym behylde apperyd; his feit, destitute of naturall myght, hyng downe, hys legg*is* cleuyd to his thyis / part of his fyngerys returnyd to the hande / restynge alwey vppon two lytyll stolys / the * quantite¹ of his body, to hym onerous / he drew aftir hym / and to the encrese of his wrecchidnesse was addyd grete pouerte / yn more afflicciou*n* to hym than his langoure : sitħ to a ma*n*e that nethir myght labur / ne goo / were witħdrawe necessaries of his lyuelode / this wrecchidnes was so mykill to hym the more greuous / that it was longe abidynge / trewly almost .xxxᵗⁱ· wynt*er* witħ this so grete A sykenes was he deteynyd / And he thus / othir witħ crepynge / othir witħ the helpe of othir² .I.-borne, sate at Londo*n*e yn the Chirche of Poulis³ / askynge almes of them that enterid yn / this I-done, nowe come the tyme acceptable / the yere of benygnyte / In the whiche Rayer hadde sette the fowndementys of his holy temple / and the fame of the newe werke / as it were a full swete odur dyffusyd by the mowthis of all the peple / it myght nat be hydde from hym / the whiche, by the mercy of oure lorde, conceyuyd a swete desire / and feitħfull / that he myght be borne to that place / ther to beeseke God of his helpe / And he, of his frendes thiddir thus borne yn a basket, felle downe a-forne the Awter / porrectynge his meke prayers to heuyn / and to the hye and glorious merltys of the blessid Apostle / alleggyng them to the hye and dredfull Iuge / that by them he myght obteyne foryeuenesse of synne And his bodyly helth / And with-owte tariynge, that welle of pyte / that was and is opy*n*e to the menstruat woma*n*e and synful man / was p*re*sent at his callyng, and a streem and Ryuer of helth and grace of hym-self made wel owte / And by and by, euery crokidnes of his body / a litill and litill losid⁴ he strecchid vn-to grownde his membris; and so anoon avawntynge hym-self vp-warde / all his membris yn naturale ordir was disposid / As it were a newe ma*n*e† he was seyn to procede forth / than howe grete a crye of them / that were present, was

* [f. 50 v.]

† [f. 51.]

¹ molem. ² vel ipse utcumque repens vel ope aliorum.
³ *in ecclesia lundoniensi beati pauli apostoli*, St. Paul's Cathedral. ⁴ dissoluta.

lyfte vp to heuyne! what terys I-schede owte for ioye / what praysyng to God, vppone soe mervelous and wondrefull myracle were yeue and payed to God / yt may bettyr be conceyued with a deuoute soule / than ex*p*ressid by worde / this dede an*oon* was
5 dyvulgate by all the Cyte. And with a grete fame. gretely accendid the peple of both ordres / the Clergie. And the laife. And frome that tyme / the noble matrones of the Cite kepte ther' nyght wacchis; the clergie and laife by companyes, fyllyn with grete deuocyone of soule / and herte gladdenes,[1] hawntyng this place.
10 and with ofte visitac*i*on solempne laude yeldid to God, with the fowndato*ur*e.

¶ CAP*ITU*LUM 14ᵐ·
¶ Of the Anthyphoner.

A Certeyne man. toke a-way a boke frome this place / that we callith an Antiphonere, the whiche was necessarie to them / that schulde synge ynne the chirche. In that,
15 specialy, that ther was nat at that tyme grete plente of bokys / yn the place / Whan it was sowghte besily. And not I-fownde / it was tellid to Rayer, the priour, what was done of thee boke, And he toke this harme with a softe herte[2] paciently. At nyghtys tyme / whan as he was ynne his chambre to take his reste, The
20 glorious Apostle of God, Bartholomew, spake to hym and seyid. "Sey, Rayer / what is that / of whoeys loste[3] / me p*r*esente, thus ye playne?" And he seied "Syr, thy clerkis hadde a profitable boke to them. In the whiche, to the honoure of God and of the / In the holy temple of thy glorie they were wownte to synge; And
25 now, yf it be hidde yn ony place or stolyne a-way / they know nat." "In[4] the mornnynge eerly, co*m*maunde thyn hors to be redy,* and hastly entre the Cite, And whane thou cu*m*myste yn to the Iewes strete[5] / spare thy sporys / lose thy brydyll, lette thyn hors to my gou*er*naunce. And yn to what howse thy hors wilfully
30 putte yne his fote / know welle of me / ther thy boke schall be fownde. Dowte no thyng; prudently and constawntly Inquyre." No more this I-seid, yn a moment he disparisshid. Rayer yn the mornynge. slyd. owte of his bedde / and diligently all that was

* [f. 51 v.]

---

[1] cordis alacritate.   [2] placida mente.   [3] cujus amissione.
[4] In the Latin the apostle's second remark is indicated by *inquit*.
[5] *vicum judeorum*, Old Jewry.

commaunde hym he executid / and with the ennemyes of pees he spake pesibly / And the boke that he sowghte he fownde / and toke hit, and brogħt hit hoome.

CAPITULUM 15ᵐ.
Of a woman i-helyd.

THe tonge of a womane so gretly was swolle that she myght nat schete here moweth. And so opynly grennyng / that sche myght nat hidde the swellynge / thys woman of her freendes was broght to this chirch, And offerid to Rayer the pryor / Whiche, hauynge compassion of her, as he was a man of mercy and grete benygnyte, offeryd to God and to his patrone prayer for her: And he, reuoluynge his relikys that he hadde of the Crosse / he depid them yn water, and wysshe the tonge of the pacient ther with. And with the tree of lyif / that ys, with the same signe of the Crosse, payntid the tokyne of the crosse vpone the same tonge. And yn the same howre all the swellynge wente his way / And the woman, gladde and hole, went home to here owne.

CAPITULUM 16ᵐ.
¶ Of a riche mane.

Hit ys tolde of a Richemane vplond dwellyng / that come to this Chirche. And he, so delitid with the gladnes of this place, And with the seruyce of God. ther contynualy and deuoutly y-doyne; he seid to the Priour, "Syr', many goodnes of this vertuous place by opyn fame * I haue knowe. And moo with myn yene I haue seyn. Wherfore .I. purpose in my soule, from this day forwarde .I. shall commytte me And all myne to seynt Barthilmewe, aduocatte of this place, And to his seruyce .I. shall me subdew / Ouerwher' calle hym and preche hym my lorde / And with my substawnce, as he wolle Inspire me / his clerkys honoure. Then seiede Rayer. "Wele thou hast purposid. And dowtles a wyse keper of thy goodes thou hast chosyne / whome yf thou serue, as thou with feithfull mynde hast promysid / withowt dowte by hym thow shalt optene the blysse of God." Aftir these wordes the mane went his way. ¶ A wondyr thyng and a worthy to be

[I. 17.]   *St. Bartholomew extinguishes a fire.*   21

remembrid : nat longe aftir, it happid hym sittynge at his table /
oone of his seruantes tolde hym that his kechyn was a-fyre
sodenly. and likly to perissh with wooddenes of fyre¹ / he was
prayd, therfore, hastly to come. And delay nat helpe to brynge to
5 the howse, nowe perysshynge and nowe fallynge. And to the
seruantes so yn soule he-stunyid² and with grete feer affrayed / the
same howseholde-fadir³ answerde / "Haue nat .I. late. me. and
myne commyttid to blessid Barthilmew the Apostle ? And hym I
haue made and deputid keper of my hede and of all thyng that
10 parteyneth to me. Yf, therfore, it plesith hym .his. to kepe / to
hym self / he shall nat nede oure helpe / but also all hole and saf,
not mynuschyd, to the solace of his seruantes, yf he be wyllyng,
hys myght .I. know wel ys sufficient ¶ Forsoith yf it be the re-
specte of the ire of God from aboue, that sendith to vs worthy
15 paynys for oure demerites / what or how moche yn withstandynge
may oure besy purpos prevayle ? / as who seyth lityll. Suffir therfore noon of vs put to his hande / lette vs abyde yn sylence / and
yn hope * the sauacyoun of God ad⁴ the myght of oure tutoure."   *[f. 52 v.
And yete as the word was yn the moweth of the speker, And at
20 the nomynacioun of the glorious Apostle / the same fyre semyd to
suffre violence / for the Flamys, naturaly ascendyng vpward /
defawtid of ther power, And vndir certeyne lymytys were restreynyd. And whane this was broght to the howsholdfadir,
beholde what he seid / "howh mykil avayleth the feith / and
25 howh emynently apperith the vertu of the Apostle / whan schulde
the impetuous flamme yeue way to oure myghtis, the whiche yn a
momente by the Apostle of God ys qwenchid / thankys of vs therfore be to hym / that as nowe, and also fro hens forwarde, wolde
wouchesafe thus to kepe vs."

CAPITULUM 17ᵐ·

¶ **Of the shippemen yn peryll.**

30 Certeyn men of the kyngis Cyte of London went owte to fer'
cowntrees. And certeyn tyme made them redy to come
home agayn with all thers. And whan they trustid them
to the wawys of the see / than blowynge of the syde the westryne

---

¹ furente incendio.   ² consternatis.   ³ paterfamilias.
⁴ In the MS. *ad*, but in the Latin *et :* a stroke representing *n* was omitted
by the scribe over the *a*.

wynde y-callid zephirus / with a swifte curse they tendid to the
desirid hauyn). And they behelde aferre, As it were þe space of .ii.
furlong*is* / the high scharpe hedis [1] owte-warde aperynge of rochis
of stoyne / by the whiche they most nedysly passe / yf it plesid
them to go further by that wey / And the maist*er* of the schippe, 5
seynge beforne grete perell to hym cummynge / yn that the
schippe with the rochis schulde be gobettemele be mynusid And
brokyne / Her' marchauntdise schulde peryssh / with the men /
and noon hope ther was of scapynge. Neu*er*theles he exhortid
them to trust yn the pyte of oure lorde. And mekely to 10
porrecte[2] to hym ther prayers / to whome nothynge ys vnpossible /
no thynge to harde / And to this seide the Londoners / "What,"
[f. 53] seide they, "drede we / men of litill * feith / the whiche haue
blessid Barthilmewe / the Doer of so grete merveles at londone;
And we haue hym at home anyhe by vs glorified, therfore / lette 15
vs p*r*ostrate oure self yn prayer to hym. And to hym with all
confidence offer oure avowys; And he, that so grete and so
shynynge benefetys. sheweth to strangers / he schall nat hyde the
bowell*is* of his mercy to his concytyseyns."[3] And whan*e*, so
prostrate, they hadde prayed to-gider, they areysyd vp from ther 20
prayer, And lokid abowte them / this way and that way. ther they
sey them self by grete space y-put of / wher, before ther prayer /
they semyd that they drewe full nye the peryl / therfore they were
gladde, and a-noon as they came to lande, they dressid[4] them to the
Chirche of the gloriouse Apostle. And .ii. tapers of grete quantyte 25
offerid for ther vowe.

¶ CAP*ITULU*M 18^{m.}

¶ Of an yonge growynge man*e*.

There was a yonge man*e*, Osberne by name, whoes right hande
clevyd to his lyfte schuldyr / his hede, compressid downe
to the hande, laye vnmevable / And nethir the hande from
the shuldyr / ne the hede from the hande myghte be dep*ar*tid / 30
this man*e*, cu*m*mynge a-forne the Auter of the blessid Apostle
Bartholomewe, with sighynge terys his mercy mekely besowght;
And he deseruyd graciously to be herde. And therfore, whan the

---

[1] cacumina. [2] porrigere. [3] concivibus. [4] se contulerunt.

fredome of his ly*m*mys were y-hadde. God, that is mervelous in his seyntes / he wit*h* alle them that wer p*r*esent, wit*h* worthy preysyng*is* magnyfied.

¶ CAP*IT*ULUM 19ᵐ·

¶ Of a womman contracte.¹

A Certeyn woman In seynte Ionys² parissh At London*e*, wit*h* longe sykenes febelid, contynuelly kepte her bedde. And, helt*h* dispeyrid / she abided only the last houre of thys lyfe / whan she herde of her neyg*h*bou*r*es / how many and howe grete thyng*is*, by the ve*r*tu of God, were do*n* yn the * Chirche of the holy Apostle / by t*h*e ve*r*tu in her conceyuyd of vnskunfitid³ feit*h* / wit*h* goode hope / she askid herself thider to be borne. And thidir whan she was .I.-browg*h*t / that she hadde herde / by experience. she provid / felynge the profit and consecutyng the effecte / of her peticiou*n* / grauntyng that / oure lorde ih*es*u cryste, the Aucto*u*r*e* of oure feit*h*, which*h* helit*h* contrite in herte and byndit*h* vp the contriciones of them.

*[f. 53 v.]

CAP*IT*ULUM 20ᵐ·

¶ Of a childe blynde from his birt*h*.

A Childe blynde from his birt*h* / oon. ledynge hym / Fadyr and modyr folowyng, was browg*h*t to the solempnyte of the glorious Apostle. And as he enteryd the chirche, he fi*ll* down*e* to the erthe, And ther a whyle turnyd hymself / now this way / nowe that way. And w*ith* tariyng restid vndir the hande of the heuenly leche that light*y*t*h* euery man*e* cu*m*mynge in-to this worlde. In whoes light a*ll* we see light. And a-noon*e* the Inward-born*e* blyndenesse fledde a-way. And the blode from the yen by the chekis down*e* rennynge / light and sight to the syke was restoryde / nat that he hadde beforne / but than first it was yeue to the childe. And than he knew his parentys wit*h* opyn*e* yen / that neue*r* he sawe beforne; And sundry thyng*is* by ther p*r*opyr namys distynctly he callide.

¹ crippled. cf. *Porta Contractorum*, Cripplegate.
² The nearest ancient parish of St. John is that in Aldersgate, now united as St. Agnes and St. Anne with St. John Zachary.   ³ invicte.

CAPITULUM 21ᵐ·

Of Wymunde that was dum.

A yonge mane, Wymund by name, yn the Courte of Eustase de Brooke / nat a litiH while y-nurysshed. Dumme he was / know to aH mene that hadde knowleche of hym / this man berynge heuyly the detrimente of his tonge / presumyng of mercy of God And one the meritys of the Apostle / he drewe 5 hym to his chirche, And ther contynually kepte deuoute wacche; And feithfully that he askid he deseruyd to obteyne / Vpone a day, aftir cumplyn, the bonde of his tonge was losyd,* and with a grete voice he praysid the vertu of the Apostle, thankynge and blessynge the myght and the wysdome of God / the whiche openyth 10 the dumme moweth / and the tongis of infantis maketh opyne and diserte.

* [f. 54]

¶ CAPITULUM 22ᵐ·

Of Godryke the Bocher.

WHan trewly the plantacioun that the hye fadyr hadde plantyd / that is to seye. the forseid chirche / whan it a-roose hyer, And the fame of the Apostolike vertu 15 euerywhere to neyghbores parfitly sownyd / and was knowen. Rayer Ioynyd to hym a certeyne olde mane, Alfun by name / to whome was sadde Age and sadnes of Age with experience of longe tyme / this same olde mane, not longe beforne, hadde bilid the Chirche of seynt Gylys, at the gate / of the Cyte / 20 that ynne englissh tonge is callid Cripilgate. And that goode worke happely he hadde endyd / Demynge Rayer this mane profitable to hym / he deputyd hym as his compayr. And with his conseH and helpe / that was for to be done disposid and parformyd / It was maner and custome to this Alfunine / with 25 mynystris of the Chirche. to cumpasse and go abowte the nye placys of the chirche, besily to seke and prouyde necessaries to the nede of the poer men / that lay in the hospitaH / and to them that were hyryd to the makynge vp of ther chirche / And that / that / was commyttid to hym / trewly to brynge home. And to sundry 30 men, as it was nede, for to deuyde / And ther was a certeyne

bocheyr, Goderyke by name, A man of grete sharpnesse / more
than semyd hym / he was a streyt man / the whiche nat oonly to
the asker wolde nat yeue / but was woonte with scornyng wordes
to ynsawt them. It fil vpone a day, that while this forsaid
5 Alfunyne wente abowte * the bochers / man / by man / And aftir   * [f. 54 v.]
othur, whan he cam to this Godryke, and mevid hym aftir the
Apostle with goode and honeste wordes, oportunely and im-
portunely, by-cause he was nat willynge to yeue / he perseueryd
stedfastly, and he wolde not go from hym voyde / And whan the
10 olde mane behelde that / nat for drede / nethir for loue of God / ne
also for mannys shame he myght not tempyr the hardnes of that
yndurat herte / from his rygoure / he brake owte yn these wordes.
" O thou vnhappy. O thou vngentle and vnkynde mane / to the
yeuer of all goodys / that for the yeiftis of heuynly goodnes wilt
15 nat comyne with the poremene of cryist / I beseche the, wrecche /
put a-way a litill and swage the hardnes of that vnfeithfull soule /
And take in experience the vertu of the glorious Apostle. yn whom
yf thou truste / I promytte the that euery pece of thy¹ [fleyssh] /
that thou yeuest me a porcion of / shall the souner be solde to
20 othir / And no thynge to the mynyssynge or lessynge of the pryce /
And what more " / He was mevyd nat with the ynstyncte or
ynward sterynge of charite, but, ouercummyn with inportunyte of
asker / he drewe owte / a peis of vilest, and castyd yt yn to his
vessell, callynge them trewantes, And bade them lightly go from
25 hym / to whom Alfunyne answerd " I shall nat go fro the / tyll my
worde and promysse be fulfilled " / And with owte tarynge / ther
was a cyteseyne couetynge to bye fleyssh / for hym and his housholde.
And of þat heip of the whiche alfunyne spake before, he boughte
atte the wille of the seller / and bare hit with hym / And whan
30 this was dywlgate by all the bocherie / for a worthy myracle, As
it was sittynge / it was take. And from that tyme / they began
to be † more prompte / to yeue ther almes / And also feruent in   † [f. 55]
deuocioun; And stryuyd who myght preuent anothir yn yeuynge /
namely / he whoes hardnes of vnfeithfull soule / the vertu of
35 cryist / hadde vndirnymyd / the whiche lorde promysid to the
ȝeuer of a dyschfull of coolde water to hym that cummyth yn the
name of a disciple, nat to lake his meide.

¹ There is space for a word after *thy* in the MS., perhaps "fleyssh" as
below (Lat.—carnium).

¶ CAPITULUM 23ᵐ·

¶ Of Eden the wyffe of Edred.

AN nothir tyme the same alfunyne, those thyng*is* that nedid to the makyng of ale, he went a-bowte to matronys howsis in cumpasse and askid / And whan he came yn-to the parissh of Seynt Giles of London*e* / for this same gaderynge / he cam yn-to a deuoute matron*e* / Eden by name / the wyf of Edred / the whiche, with meruellus deuocion), louynge cryistis Apostle / her almes to his chirche / or els she broughte / or els was wonte to sende yt : to whom cum*m*ynge Alfunyne, he prayed her of her blessyng / that sumwhat sche wolde departe with hym / for the loue of God / And sche answerd that she hadde but oonly .vii. Ceves ful of malte. And she shulde take a-wey ony thyng / of these / she myghte nat than / parforme the brethen¹ / that she hadde begun*n*e / "Neu*er*-the-lees," she saide / "Albe that .I. be / certeyn*e* to haue damage or harme / yete hadde I leuer to suffir harme of myn ale / than yow to go voyde with-owte frute of myn Almes " / thus seyynge / she mesurid one cevefull And yaue it to the mynystris / the whiche passynge forthe and I-go / she began to mesure that remaynyd / And wondir to seye, .vii. mesures she fownde / the whiche her-self trowynge to haue errid in numberynge / began to telle ageyn*e*. And than she fownde .viii. The thirde tyme she num*m*berid, and fownde .ix. And than at the * foureth metynge fownde .x. Beholde þ*at* she, þ*at* studied to fulfill the plenytude of the lawe / that is charite / of the rightwys rewarder, for her mede, fownde .x. The which woman / that / that / remanyd so habowndynge / commawndid to be borne to the same chirche / anoyn / And tolde eue*r*ywhere the mervelous encresse / blessynge God, that by his seyntes workith tokenys And v*er*tues, to whom, whan he wolle, myghte is redy.

¶ CAPITULUM 24ᵐ·

¶ De godena contracta.²

A Certeyn*e* woman, Godene by name / hadde her leggis returnyd to her thyys, that neu*er* myght stonde vpright / but with contynuall vse of sittynge ledde a tedious lyfe / yn sorowe

---

¹ cervisiam. ² *contracta*, the cripple.

and wepynge she one a tyme was borne to the Chirche of the blessid Apostle / and askid the yifte of parfit helth, And obteynyd it / grauntynge þat oure lord ihesu criste, the whiche losith stokkid men / reysith vp downe pressid / And directith the rightwys.

CAPITULUM 25ᵐ·

¶ Of a man that myght not slepe.

A Certeyn man at Norwiche, opynly I-know [1] / while one a tyme he wolde be lette blode And of hym self toke noon hede / as it was expedient / hadde lost the rest of slepe / the whiche, how good & how necessarie it is to man / for to expowne it is nat now necessarie / this reste / longe and dayly sweitis and laboures allightith / And aftyr labur, repayrith man aʒeyne to labour / and this reste, not onely of men, but of bestis conseruyth the nature sownde and hole. The sayed wrecchid man lackynge this rest, ledde one nyghtys withowte slepe almost .vii yere. And by and by / his senowys were contracte, pale and lene / and ryvelyd abowte the moweth all discolouryd / And all his bonys to be numbryd Apperid, to the sight of them that byhelde hym / And to the heip [2] and * encrece of his greve and febylnes, was putte to nedynesse; so moche that the mane beforne was riche yn frendes & money / And nowe, of bothe destitute, he was applied to ydelnes. For nethir to hym-self, nethir to his / myght he ony thynge prouyde. In .vii. ʒeire of his vnfortune / whan the relikys of the same chirche of seynt Batholomewe / were browght and put yn / to the oratorye of sente Nicholas [3] at ʒermoweth / this man drewe to the same relykys deuoutly / And mekely prostratte hymself. askyng and sekynge remedy. And he fownde that he sowght / he range at the doyr / and oure porter opynde to hym / and shewid to hym magnyfycently the bowellis of his mercy / And grovelynge to the grownde, he multiplied his prayers, and began to slepe. And whan he hadde slepte a grete while, he roys vpe hole / And wente to his owne / yeldynge thankynges to God / that mortifieth and revyuyth / smytyth and helyth.

* [f. 56]

[1] notissimus. [2] ad cumulum.
[3] The parish church of Yarmouth is dedicated to St. Nicholas.

¶ CAPITULUM 26ᵐ·

Of a dum childe.

Also a childe that longe tyme was dumme. to the laude of the glorious Apostle / the vertu of God opynde both tonge and moweth, and rightwesly he spake.

¶ CAPITULUM 27ᵐ·

¶ Of an othur, callid Nychalas.

A Childe faire of fourme. nicholas by name. so had he his legge so strecchid forth / to the vpper parties of his thyy / that he myght nat putte yt forward ne drawe yt bakewarde / yn asmoche that the synowys were dryed vp. And alweys lackid bowablenesse / he, therfore, lenyng on a staffe, vsid that yn stede of his fote / this childe cummynge to the Chirche of the blessid Apostle Bartholomew, was expert that oure lorde is full sweytt to al men / And his mercy ys abouyne all his workys / by the merites of the most glorious Apostle / hete of lyf was ynfowndid to seyr and drye membrys, And anoon * folowid full helth / the whiche chylde abided ther a while, And seruyd the Chanons ther / yn ther kychyne, And for the yifte of his helth / he yaue the seruyce of his body.

* [f. 56 v.]

¶ CAPITULUM 28ᵐ·

¶ Of Adwyne the carpenter.

AN nothir mane, Alfunyne by name, in the towne of Dunwych,[1] that dwellid one the see syde / So was contracte that he myghte not vse the free office / nethir of hande / ne of fote / his leggis were cleuynge to the hynder parte of his thyes / that he myghte nat goo / and his handis turnyd bakewarde / no thynge with them myght be do / ne worke / the extremyteis of his fyngers were so rigorisly contracte in the synowys / that he myght vnneith put mete to his moweth.[2] In this greuous

---

[1] In Suffolk.   [2] vix ori escas porrigebat.

sykenes he passid his yonge age. And whane he attayned to
mannys age, and not yette hadde he power of his lymmys / yette,
sith the fame of tokenys and myracles of the blessid Apostle come
to hym by relacioun of othir men / he began to leyfte vp his sorow-
5 full soule in-to a better hope. And thow helth were yn that tyme
dilaid / it was promysed to come // Therfore / for that he was ferre
from that chirche / he yaue shipmen for hyr hyyr, and by shippe
he was browght to the chirche / and put yn the hospitall of pore
men. ¶ And ther a while of the almes of the same chirche
10 y-sustenyd / And he began yn the meyn while / by the vertu of
the Apostle, to take breith vnto hym / And [t]he¹ desirid helth² /
by certeyne incrementys began to come Ageyne. ¶ First with handys,
thow they were crokyd, he dyd make smale workys, as disstafes /
and antell³ / and othir wommenys instrumentys / And forthermore
15 by successioun, whan othir membrys vsyd ther naturall myghte, he
folowid yn greter workys / hewerrys of wode with axe and
* squarerys of tymbyr with chippynge axe⁴ / and nat longe aftir * [f. 57]
the crafte of carpentrye / yn the same chirche, and yn the Cite of
Londone he excercisid / as it hadde be taught hym / from his
20 childehode / blessynge God. whoes yen / be oone them / that
dredith hym / And vppon them that hope one his mercy.

¶ CAPITULUM 29ᵐ·

¶ Of a dropyk mane.

A Certeyne dropik mane / that bare his surname of the happe⁵
of this siknes / myght nat hyde away his ynwarde greyf /
but to the sight of vttir beholders / he shewyd owte his
25 greyf and wracchidnys soithly / an humur reynnynge vndir the
skyne made a bollnyng inflacion, and the wombe swellyng owte /
shewid owtwarde / what pestilence was hydde ynward. thys mane
was browght to the chirche of seynt Bartholomew / but for the
gretnes of his doloure / he was turmentid / and in-to dyuers parties

---

¹ MS. he. ² et optata sanitas. ³ pensa, weights.
⁴ cesores lignorum securi et dolabra magnis operibus imitabatur.
⁵ eventu.

he walowid hymself yn the pament:[1] And at the last, yn the sight of all men he cast owte wondir venym. And his ynwardes were purgid from this dedly fylthe, and, all hole, ret*u*rnyd to his Awne howse.

[1] in diversas partes se in pavimento volutando torqueret.

¶ HERE ENDITH THE FIRSTE BOKE.

¶ SECUNDUS LIBER.

And here begynneth the Prolog of the secunde.

TO vs confessynge to God. And bigynnynge to telle his mervels / we truste feithfully he shall yeue a goode endynge / the whiche hath yeue a goode begynnynge. Nowe rennyth to oure mynde one solempne thynge / to be seied for
5 many ; And whan this hath be movyd / both by opyn / resunne / and vnyuersall wytnes / more licencyous we may passe yn-to othir / y-done by like vertu / and evyn power'. ¶ Hedirto we haue writyn examplys of myracles / the whiche were done / In the dayes of goode remembrawnce of Rayer, Priore & foundatoure * of   *[f 57 v.]
10 this place / to the laude of God / and excitament of holynes And nowe it is for to do and procede of these thyngis that we han seyn and herde done in the dayes and tymes of the successoures / of the forsaide priore. The gret solempne thynge ys thys. ¶ First, whan the rememberid priour was ȝit a-lyue / the whiche
15 edified the frame of this precious worke vpon the fowndament of Appostles and prophetys / For as moche as the bygynnyngis of grete thyngis / nedith gretter helpe / thanne most was prompte, and presente haunttid, plenty of mynystryd grace from God / Furthermore, those than aftir to the avowers / that the celestiall
20 fadir drewe yn to the odur' of his oynnementys, renvydde a newe solempnyte / of them / that ranne to religioun with an ynwarde newydde deuocyoun. ¶ Also a newe solempnyte was for obuencyouns and ȝiftes. In money / In howseholde / In corne / and in meveable goodis / grete nowmbyr. And than aftir a Ioconde
25 feiste / bisy in this place was hadde of recouerynge men yn to helthe / of them that langwysshid / of drye men, of contracte men ¹ / of blynde men / dome men / and deif men / For these causys, whan the day of his natyuyte In-to heuyn was knowyn, yt was solempnyzed and honourid with grete myrth and dawnsynge
30 yn erth. And men presydde hydder' thykly, for variawnte causys / and shuldrid to-gider, And as languyshynge men were there, abidynge the mevyng of the water of grace / that yn a

---

¹ *of contracte men,* not in the Latin MS.

certeyn place / as this same / And yn certeyne tyme, they shold presume / and truste well the wonte grace / to be ȝeuen to them / as was beforne to othyr. As the dayly relikys of them. Preche and schew to vs // And this is that / that we seide beforne / oone solempne for many.* or els many to make one solempne feiste. 5 For as the blesside kyngdome of israel / all was / as it hadde be one proficye of cryste and of his chirche, So al these thyngis that bene seide or shall be seide / they beholde the ende / and consummacioun of this document / For trewly God is yn this place / And though ther be non place with-owte hym / the whyche God, 10 yn place ys not comprehended, nothir mesurid / nat for the place these be doone oonly. but for man / For the whiche bothe mane & place is reuerencid / Neuerthelese, ther is no so preuy mane of crystis secretys / that may contempne the reuerence of holy place, whiche deputat ys only to dyuyne vse / And consecrate ys to the remedye 15 of soulys / where oure holy thyngis be put / wher is the distribucioun of the sacramentis / And wher that is / that is most beste / the presence of crystis body / nat withoute experience of his vertuys / with grete office of angely mynystracyoun / and with solempne worschipe of deuocyoun of all seyntes / Dredefull, ther- 20 fore, is this place to the vnderstander / ther is no thyng her els / but the howse of God and the gate of heuyn / to the beleuer. Trewly, they that byleue nat ne vndirstonde not by charite yn beleuyuge of these mysteryes / but scornyth oure Sabatte dayes / and poluteth oure halowys that clensyn othir men / we schall take them / as men 25 transfiguryng them-self / yn to an Angell of lighte, thowgh they be darke bodyes. demyng pyte to be feynyd for lucre / and so they sholde be takyn till the consummacioun of synne, antecryste / shall come / whan the erthe shall be take vnto wykkid men / And halowys yn-to conculcacioun / that they may be opyn than, that 30 now be hydde yn the denne of theyfes. Spirituall,† sothly, seyntwary / that heir ys bilid / of qwyke stonys. A bilynge certeynly styddefastly here permanent, vnspottid shall be translatid yn-to the kyngdome euerlastynge; And as yn the erthly Empyr vnsittynge it is / And suspecte, any man excepte only oone persone / 35 to schewe knyghthode yn his propre name / we haue oone of these that oure Lorde hathe ordeynyd prynces vppone erthe / We haue, as I seye / the doer of mervels, oure patrone / and Duke / seynt Bartholomew / whom, by the grace that he hath plentwesly receyuyd of cryste / we beseke hym / that / with his myghty 40

Death of Rahere.

Auctorite / that commendeth the vertu of his mayster. vs aftir hym nat oonly he wolde lede, but also that he drawe and heigge¹ oure wayes with thornys / that we go nat after the desires of oure fleshe. ¶ And with fadirly chastynge / compelle vs to entre the soper of the Lambe, And the euerlastyng mariage of hym / that takith awey the synnys of the worlde; the whiche peticioun he vouychesafe to ȝeue vs, the whiche lyuyth and reigneth God / per all worldes, with-owtyne ende, Amen.

ALSO ANOTHIR.²

Also, as we be lernyd of worldly kunnynge / As it were by the spoylys of egipcyanys / the office of a necligent man is / nat to know the begynnyngis of his werkys / nethir to charge the endyngis / gretly yn vs it semyth reproueable / that ar lernyd men / nat to know the grownde and the resone of them / that we worschippe / Moyses, sothly, that fyrst taught vs / to spoyle the egipcians, he taught vs how we shulde answere to oure aftir cummers / askyng vpone oure sacramentis / what they wolde meyn, seyng thus / for to signyfie to them / the religion of the same. Therfore, aftir the ȝerys * of his prelacie .xxii.³ and .vi. monthes / the .xxᵗʸ. day of Septembre the .vii. moneth, The cley howse of thys worlde he forsoke / and the howse euerlastynge he enterid / that fowndid this howse, in-to the laude and honoure of þe name of cryst, that yn the howse of hys fadir he myght be crownyd / yn his myildnes / and yn his mercyes. And in as mykil⁴ as of no workys with-owte charite cummyth forth profeite / with-owte whiche charite / othir goodys may not prevayle⁵ / the whiche also charite may nat be hadde with-owte othir goodys / by the whiche man is made goode. Rightly so we of hym haue this hope, that no thynge hath he omysid by hym that tochith grace / of that that we seke here in thys passyng lyfe / as is the communyon of crystes feith / And communycacioun of his sacramentis, and namly insignys of a contrite herte by penaunce / For why. Amonge

* [f. 59]

---

¹ sepiat, hedge.   ² Item aliud.
³ XXII. This would make Rahere begin his priorate, March 1123, as the manuscript implies, and would give September 20, 1144, as the day of his death. The Latin reads "Igitur post annos prepositure XXII.os et menses sex vigesimo die sept' septi mensis relicta domo lutea." As Easter day in 1144 was on March 26, September was the seventh month in that year.
⁴ asmykil, as much.   ⁵ MS. pro for pre.

these we trust that he passid / And yn thys we trust / as we hope
in the meritorie helpe of oure myghty patrone / to whom the litil
flokke of .xiii. Chanouns / as a few sheippe he hath lefte with
litil lande / and right fewe rentys / Neuerthelese, with copious
obuencyons of the Awter', and helpynge of the nygh parties of the 5
populous Cyte, they were holpyn / Sothly they florysch now / with
lesse fruite than that tyme / whan the forsayd solempnytees of
myracles were excercysyd by a lykewyse / As it were a plante whan
yt is wele y-rotyd / the ofte wateryng of hym cesith. The tyme of
a 3ere turnyd abowte / succedid in-to the prepositure and the 10
dignyte of the priore of this new plantacioun, admyttid by the
bysshope of Londone, lorde Robert[1] / Thomas,[2] oone of the
* [f. 59 v.] Chanouns of the chirche * of seynt Osyth,[3] the 3ere of oure Lorde
M^{mo}. and C^{mo}. and xliiij^{ti}. the sevyne indiccioun[4] / reignynge
Stevyne / the sone of Stevyne / Erle blesence[5] / the whiche 15
promouyd. Theobalde[6] beccence / in-to the Archebisshope of
Cawntirbery. This Thomas, as we haue prouyd in comyn / was
a man of iocunde companye / and felowly iocundite, of grete
eloquence / And of grete cunnynge, instruct in philosophy / And
dyuyne bokys exercisid / and he hadde yt in prompte / what 20
sumeuer he wolde vttir / to speke yt metyrly / And he hadde
in vse euery solempne day, whan the case requyrid / to dispense
the worde of God / And, flowynge to hym the prees of peple /
he 3aue & so addid to hym glorie vtward, that ynward hadde
3eue hym this grace / He was prelate to vs mekly almost .xxx^{ti}. 25
3ere / And in Age An hundrid wyntir almost / with hole wyttis /
with all crystyne solempnyte / tochynge crystes grace, he decessid,
and was put to his fadres / the 3ere of oure Lorde. M.C.lxxiiij.
Of the Papassie of blesside Alexawndir the third .xv. 3ere[7] / of the
coronacioun of the most vnskunfitid kynge of Englonde, Henry 30
the secunde .xx.^{ti} 3ere[8] / the xvij. day of the moneth of Ianyuer /
In the same 3ere of the eleccion of Lorde Richard,[9] Archbysshope

[1] Robert de Sigillo, Bishop of London, 1141-1151.
[2] Thomas was therefore elected Prior about September 1141.
[3] St. Osyth in Essex : a house, like St. Bartholomew's, of Augustinian
canons, founded by Richard de Belmeis, Bishop of London, the friend of
Rahere.
[4] The seventh indiction is A.D. 1144.   [5] *Blesence*, of Blois.
[6] Theobald, Abbot of Bec, in Normandy, elected Archbishop, Dec. 13,
1138.   He died April 18, 1161.
[7] *I.e.* 1174.   [8] *The xx. of Henry II.*, 1173-74.
[9] Richard, prior of Dover, was consecrated Archbishop of Canterbury April
8, 1174.   The year 1174 began March 24, and ended April 12.

of Cawntirbery, Aforne whom oure brethrene were put and sette,
of hys goode grace hym praynge / whom the grace of God from
the forsayid paucyte / encresid yn-to .xxxv.ᵗᵒ Encresyng' with
them temperaH goodes euynly. the whiche the ȝeuer of aH goodys
promysid to be cast to them / that sekith the kyngdome of God /
In this mannys tyme grewe the plante of this Appostolike branche
yn glorie ⸝ And grace before God / and man / and with moor'
ampliat* bylyng / were the skynnys of oure tabernaculys dylatid /
to the laude and glorie of oure Lorde ihesu criste, to whom / be /
honoure / and glory / worlde with-owtyn ende.   Amen.

*[f. 60]

¶ *CAPITULUM PRIMUM* 2ⁱ. *LIBRI*.

Of a deyf mayde, dum, blynde, and contracte.

THe ȝere from the incarnacioun of oure Lorde .M.C.xlviij.
aftir the obite / of Harry the first, kynge of Englonde,[1] the
xij. yere / whan the goldyne path of the son / reducid to vs
the desirid ioyes of festfuH celebrite / than with a newe
solempnyte / of the blessid Apostle, was yllumynyd with newe
myracles this holy place.   Langwissyng' mene greuyd with variant
sorys / soiftly lay yn the chirche with schynynge lightys / prostrate /
besekynge the mercy of God / and the presence of seynt Bartholomew.   And certeyne the longe mercy of God / was not fer
fro them, the whiche alway is present to the vowis of feithfuH
besekers.   Sum man ioyed with voyce of Iubilacion / that he
hadde receyuyd remedie of his akynge hede / An nothir for
reparacioun of his goyng / that he lackyd / An nothir from
ryngyng of his erys / thys man was free from corrupcioun of
lymmys / This mane putte a-syde bleriednes of yen,[2] and ioyid the
clerenes of sharpe sight receuyd / Many other men ioyid to be
swagid from the vexacioun of feverys / ȝeuynge thanke to the
honoure of the Appostle.   Certeyne whyle euerywhere / for suche
thyngis was ȝeue applause and gladenes of aH the peple / In the
lyfte corner of the Chirche / of sum men was herde wepyng and
waylyng, where lay a certeyne DamseH deyf and dumm, lackyng
sight of boeth yen / and with returnyd leggis contract, whoes

---

[1] Henry I. died December 1, 1135. So that these events took place in the year 1147.   [2] occulorum lippitudine.

parentys waylynge lay grovelynge / to the / pauyment / And cesid
not from prayer / tyl aƚƚ thyng / * was fynyschid of the clergy /
that was expedient / to so grete a feste / It plesid therfore the
goodnes of god / to condescende to ther peticiouns / And not
furthermore his creature of the maliciouſ power to be vexid / but from 5
euery bownde of syknes fully and p*a*rfitly to be delyue*r*yd /
therfore whan the Chanouns sange the secunde euynsonge / the
mayde begane greuously to be turmentyd / and sorer than she was
woonnte to be vexid / frotyng at the moweth̄ / smytynge her
breste. and betynd her' hede / a-ȝenste the grownde / trewly. 10
Whane they come to the ympne of oure blessid lady / that the
Altarys shulde be yncensid / the forsaid mayde began with̄ a sharpe
voyce to crye / and her membrys with̄ a grete myght̄ she strecchid
owt / Anoon ioyfuƚƚ skippyng forth̄ / here yen now newe / And
now clere / with̄ the lynnyn clothe / that she was clothid yn / 15
wypyd them / and dryed them / and thus with̄ stedfast stondyng /
whan she was repayrid of heryng / and of the acceptable light̄ of
seyng so gracyously receyuyd / she ran to the table of the holy
Awter / spredyng owte both̄e handys to heuyn / And so she that a
litiƚƚ be-forne was dum / now ioyng in laude of god p*a*rfitly sowndyd 20
her word*is* And to her parentys ther for ioye wepynge / plenteously
affirmyd her-self free from aƚƚ maner of syknes.

CAP*I*TULUM 2ᵐ.
Of A childe delyueryd owte of bondys.

Hit happid one a tyme that a pore mane for to bye his
vitayles / cam to londone / also his wyfe to sustene ther
pore lyfe. was wount also. from the contray cume to the 25
Cite / to receyue her wagys / for that she hadde sponne / thys pore
mane with̄ his wyf hadde yn custome euery ȝere to visite the place of
Seynt Bartholomew with̄ his offerynge / and mekly † commend
hym-self to the holy relikys of the same chirch̄. The olde serpent
ennemy to aƚƚ mankynde / the whiche eue*r* is besy / to deuoure / 30
or els to troble / the pees of feith̄fuƚƚ men / enviynge the tranquyllite
of these man and woman And the honest pouerte / he suggestid
to A certeyn bayly / of his by-synne that he shulde pretende /
to the forseide pore man leynge awayte and aspyes / he

roos therfore erly / yn the mornnynge / this gylfuH mane, namyd
Alureid / the bedyl or forcryer / and leyid wacche, as a rampawnde
lyon, aʒenst the pore man / ther was no taryng / but the ynnocent
and the theyf meitt / And whan this gallowus man toke hym
5 by the skyrtis / of his palle or mantyl / he cryed vppon hym
horriblely / vndir-nymdid hym, and reprevid hym of thefte / and
smytte hym wykkidly with his fyste / seiynge / "Wher be thy
mersmentis / that thou by theifte hast take away / deceyuyng the
mynystrys of the Shereve with drawyng tol a thowsand tymes?"
10 And whan the pore mane arayed hym to Answere / ther come
rennynge to hym / many of the same gylefuH felschipe accusynge
the ynnocent / they smytte hym / they trode hym vndir fote /
they bownde hym / and yn captyuyte led hym to pryson; And
whan they come to the howse of this forcryer or bedyl / or, y may
15 say, of that robber / they bownde hym with fetterys / beit hym
with scorgys / askyng of hym that he hadde nat, that is to say,
gret quantyte of money. At the last, wery of betyng / they put
abowte his necke a coller of Iren / of grete weighte, and a grete
chayne on othir parte / of the Inner towre / rennyng thorow the
20 myddyl of the wallys, that they myghte kepe hym more surly / and
fastnyd the ende * of the cheyne / with a staake / thus this wrecche   * [f. 61 v.]
withowt remedye, withowt mercy / yn wepynge & sighynge / in
colde / and brosynge drayf forth many dayes. Vpon a day whane
of custome, the chanons of the chirche of seynt Bartholomewes
25 a-fore the mornynge / the matens endid / and began to synge
Te deum laudamus. And the peyH of beH was roonge / the forsayed pore mane, the whiche was artid in bondys / herynge the
sownde of the bellis / and the melodye of ympnys /—the howse
sothly, that he was crucyat yn. was nygh by to the chirche /—
30 And he began with deuoute soule and lamentable voice to crye /
and, as he cowde or myght, to calle vpone seynt Bartholomewe /
¶ Whane he hadde so done Intently and ofte / he deseruyd to
haue the affecte of his feithfuH peticioun, And felt now / nat as
before, hym-self so chargid with ferramentis and Iryns / wher-
35 fore, leftynge vp handys and armys, he fownde hym-self I-losid /
And skippynge forth with all Iryne machynamentis / he came to
the doer, and fownde yt opyne. And whan the grete chayne and
coller of Iryn & of the fetterys grete payse / that he bare, made so
grete a noyse / the forsaide Alurede sodaynly awakid / skippid
40 owte of his bedde / and with a swyft paase folowid / Anoone, as

he was owte / And his fugityue by the mone-light sawh / he wolde
a folowid hym, and he wolde a cried / but thorow the wylle of
God / nethir he myght meve his fote, nethir breke owt with his
voyce. So the pore mane, skapyng by seynt Barthilmew help,
And with a grete ioye enterynge his chirche / prostrayt hym-self
afore the holy Auter of the Apostle, makyng knowlegge that by
his helpe he was delyuered / yeldyng to God / and hym thankyngis
/ And tolde to them / that stoid abowte / the ordir of the benefeit
I-ȝeuen to hym.

¶ CAPITULUM 3ᵐ·

¶ Of shippemen yn grete peryll.

CErteyn marchawntis, hauyng ther Shippis stuffid with nesses-
saries to howseholde / with hope of lucur' commyttid them-
self to the meveable wyndis / and vncerteyn see / purposyng
to londone to eschange with encreys of the marchawntdise / sothly
whane they were meuyd from the porte of flawndrys / and with
swifte course bygan to passe thorow the see / the light of the son
was closid yn derke clowdys, And the eyr' was changid, and began
to be fulle of stormys / and thonderynge horrible / All the elementys
pretendid to the wrecchid shipmene deith of nature / And whan,
a litil a-forne, .xi. schippis fro the havyn of the pesible porte /
with ioye ther shulde be losid / A mervelous happe and a lamentable caase / In a breyf space / with the wodnes of wynde / euery
of them were cast from othir / ther was amonge othir / one grete
schippe amonges them / that were yn peryll / with so grete a
violence of contrary wynde so smyt / ¶ And festnyd yn the derke
sandys / that as mykil as it was yn mannys knowlege / stode to
the myddis yn the sande / Neuerthelese ther was oone a-monge
the wepers and waylers & mystrustres ripyr & sadder of age,
whiche, with a meke and contryte herte / offerynge sacrifice to
God, seid ".I. warne yowe / ouercumme in labour / and now here
felowis of peryll / vnto this tyme / that the goodnys of God hath
be mercyfull to vs / Lette not vs be vnkynde / to the precedent
meritis of oure former ¶ Lette vs prayse oure maker for the
perceyuyd ȝiftis of affluent grace / And also for this euylles that
we suffre iustly oure demerytys requyrynge / lette vs take hit with

a pacient soule. Now, now, as ye se / stonditħ yn to vs / thᵃ day of oure Iugement. Now / wil we / Nul we / we be come for oure synnys to the butte and terme or marke of vniuersaH kynde of man. ¶ Neuertheles / O you men, trust ye / ȝit remaynytħ
5 hope / and ȝit here ther is place of foryeuennesse / and God may delyuer vs from oure peryH : noo cowhseH artyth hym / noo thyng excluditħ he from them / that callitħ vpone hym yn trewitħ / And yn tyme of angwyssh / whoes dyuyne wiH / eternally preceditħ euery creature / his dignyte transcenditħ and his power dispositħ /
10 Lette vs confesse to hym oure synnys / Lette vs shewe to hym the nakidnes of oure synfuH nature / lette vs now or neuer / begyne to be ashamyd / of the wykkidnes of oure shamefuH conuersacioun / lette vs calle to vs the Citycens of the heuenly courte / and beseke the helpe of the blessid modir of God, Marye / that she
15 peys to vs the kynge of eternaH glorie / And ȝit ther is a litiH space / I beseke you with oo sowyl to here : And ȝe here me paciently now, now / it shaH be opyne to you / the way of heltħ / the porte of iocundite / the gate of youre delyuerawnce / .I. haue herde specialy of oo seynt / an heuynly cityseyn / ¶ I haue herde
20 of seynt Barthilmewe, that a-monge the knyghtis of the heuynly kynge ys worthy to be callid vppone, whiche plesawntly con-descenditħ to the prayers of deuoute askers / therfor lette vs offer oure vowys to so grete a patrone, that it may plese hym / by hys prayers to delyuer * vs, And oure shippe witħ marchawñdyse / Lette   * [f. 63]
25 vs, therfore, lyfte vp oure handis to heuyn. / And avowe witħ clere deuocioun that whane we cum whidir we purpose to Lundone / we shaH bere thedir / in the honoure of seynt Barthilmewe, a Shippe of syluer / aftir the fourme of oure Shippe / made on) oure costys and collecte or gaderyng maade amongse vs / offerynge yt
30 to that chirche yn mynde of oure delyueraunce." ¶ Vnneitħ he cesid of speche / that al men ther togidir helde vp an higħe ther handys / and made ther vowys / callyng one seynt Barthilmewe / And nat yn ydle / Al men trewly by-holdyng, and the houre of the nygħe deitħ abidynge : presente was seynt Barthilmewe
35 mercyfully / And with his holy hande drewe fortħ the shippe / by the for ende / the whiche, goynge fortħ witħ his wounte pase² / in the ouer party¹ of the see comme in-to the streym / and was delyueryd from the sandys / than, at the laste, aH were gladde / And,

---

¹ superficie.   ² solido passu.

blowynge a goode wynde, they come to the porte of the desired
cyte / And so they, goynge owt of the Shippe, that litiłł shippe,
forgyd and made of siluyr, ioyfully they bare / to the chirche of
the holy Apostle / And to the prior I-callid, with summe of his
Chanouns / they tellid the processe of ałł this storie / yeldynge 5
thankys to almyghty God / And to the glorious Apostle And
martir, seynt Barthilmewe.

¶ CAPITULUM 4ᵐ·

¶ Of the oratory of oure lady.

IN the eeste parte of the same chirche / ys an Oratory¹ / and yn
that / An Awter' yn the honoure of the most blessid / and
parpetuałł virgyne mary y-consecrate. ther was in the con- 10
gregacioun of those brethreṅ / a certeyn man, Hubert by / name /
cumme of grete kyne / informyd yn liberałł science / of goode age
and of wondirfułł myldenes / that yn his² / ałł thyng * worldly /
hadde forsake / for the loue of criste / nakidly askapynge the wrake
of this worlde / And the habite that he did one of holy religion / 15
with feithfułł maners worshipfully he bewtified / Whan he was
admyttid in-to the feleshippe of brethrene, he turnyd ałł his study
to loue God / and to prayer / and redynge bysyly toke hede / and
many that were his elders / he passid yn rightwysnes / and trewth.
this mane yn the forsayde oratorye / afore the holy Awter' ofte 20
prostrate hym self / and offerid hym self / a loveable and qwyke
hooste, in-to odure of swetnesse to God / and to his blessid modir.
To this mane a-monge praynge yn the same place / sumtyme
apperid / the modyr of mercy / seiyng with a hony and swete
moweth "Chanons," she sayed, " of this chirche, thy bretheryn / 25
my derlyngis / yn this place consecrate to my name / sumtyme
payid to me solempne office of massys / and deuoute seruyce / of
feithfułł reuerence ʒeif to me / And now hath vndircrept them
necligence / charite chyillith, that nethir heir' the holy mysterys of
my son be hawntid, nethir to me. wounte praysyng of them be 30
ʒeuyn / therfore, from the highe descense of heuynnes, by the
consent of my son, hedir .I. descende / for the ʒeuyn obsequy of

---

¹ This is the Lady chapel of which traces remain under the late Fringe
Factory. ² Latin MS. senectute.

[* f. 63 v.]

honoure to ȝeue thankys / and for the necligence to vndirnym and
reprove / and for to warne my derlyngis. Heerʾ, sothly, prayers
and vowys of them .I. shall receyue, and mercy and blisse .I. shall
yeue to them euerlastyngʿ" / thus she seyed, And from the sight
5 of hym sodanly dysperyshid. He that these wordys herde / opynly
expressid them to hys bretheryn. And yn-to the seruyce of the
modir of God made them moore prompte and feruent / O ! wyth
what reuerence / with what feithfull and swete* affeccioun / ys that *[f. 64]
place worthy to be worshippid / whiche ys so holy / wher the
10 shynynge Queyn) of heuyne / the lady of the worlde / the modir
and the most cleene spowse of the eternall kynge / hath vouchesayf
to shewe herʾ propre presence / and to the puttyng forth & praysyng
of her name / mercyfully hath excited, with plesaunte exhortacioun
repellynge the sloweth of herʾ seruantys.

¶ CAPITULUM 5ᵐ.

¶ Of a certeyne clerke.

15 IT happid yn a Towne that ys callid enfelde¹ / beestis to dye /
with harde & sodayne pestlence / the whiche pestlence was
causid / of the corrupcioun of the ayre / or els, as we bettir
trow / for to noye man to his amendment / ȝeuen of God from
aboue / hit did grete harme yn townys neir adiacent ; also þer was
20 a-mong þem a certeyn clerk, a louer of treweth And equyte / that
lyk vnfortune lyke harm had sufferid / ix. of his oxys with this
pestilence weere slayne.   And a yonge hefker alone. Leuyng.
Lay yn thryssheholde, lyke deithe as the othur abidynge. The
seied clerk þes thingis consideryng, seied þes wordis. "Lo ! ourʾ
25 synnes askyng the vnmercy of oure Lordys ire / howgh yt commyth
vppone vs / and the bestys that bene ordeynyd / to the vse of
man / by / and by dyen / this is expedient vs for to do / that be-
tweyne oure squorgyng ȝeue we thankyngis. to God / In that God
ȝeuyth / & God takyth / and as it plesith God / so it is done /
30 blessid be the name of God. ¶ In that / this clensyng scourge /
may be withdrawe from vs / And this pestlence furthermore attayn
nat / to oure bowndys / this hefker / that is oonly leyfte to me /
ȝyf it leue, .I. a-vowe yt to be sent to the chirche / of most blessid

¹ Enfield, Middlesex, ten miles north of London.

Barthylmewe the Apostle / that by his glorious prayers / may be turnyd from vs / the respect of * Goddis yndignacioun / And ȝyf this beist dye / whan the skyne shall be takyne from the fleshe, and I haue solde hit, .I. shall make the pryse / to be sent / to the same chirche." / In the meyn whyle / A marchaunte was at hande 5 / with whom the clerke began to treit of sale of this beist / demynge it shulde not escape the peryll of deith / And whyle they alterid to-gidir, the hefker areis / uppe hole / and sownde / and begane to ete of þe hey that was by / And the clerke, this be-holdyng / Anoone payed his vowe, And sent this hefker to this 10 forsayd chirche / with goode hope made full gladde that oure lorde, by the merytis of the glorious Apostle / hadde accepte his vowe and his prayer.

CAP*ITULUM*. 6ᵐ·

¶ Of a calf heuenly y-markyd yn bothe erys.

A Certeyne womane dwellynge beside the castell of Mun-fychet,[1] ledyd an holy lyif, and thow she stode yn the 15 bonde of mariage / as it was vs seyid / she yaue her soule to contynence, and with prayers and abstynence did her devir God to plese / she hadde a cowe with calfe, the whiche, by tokenys owtwarde, drewe neir to calvyng ; And stondyng neyr the tyme that the fruyt shulde be proferid forth / the cowe begane inwardly 20 with throwys to be tormentyd / hugely / that it was trowid to suffir deith / that beholdyng, this deuoute woman seyid to her seruantys / "yf the glorious apostle Barthilmewe, of his wount pite, wyll restore to vs oure cowe hole / the calfe that she bryngeth forth / we shall marke yt one the ere / And diligently norysche 25 hit ; And whan it is wenyd, I shall sende yt to his chirche." / And with-owt taryng, whan all therto was assentynge / the doloure was swagid / the fruyt / was forth broght / and a mer*velous thyng, And a nouelte wondirfull there nowe happid / the calfe that newly was browght forth yn-to the light / from his modir-is 30 wombe / hadde boith endes of his erys kyt of / And the same tokyne and marke that the woman seied beforn) she wolde make yn one ere / apperid y-made yn boith. ¶ And hauynge no tokyne of the wonde newe / but as a thynge hadde be kut of / And helid

[1] The Castle of Mountfichet, finally destroyed in 1276, was near Blackfriars.

a3eyn / so vestige apperid / who was the doer / or with what
instrument thei were kut / we commyt that to hym / that serchid
the deyp secretes of man,[1] to whom is no thynge harde / no thynge
ympossible / they wondrid aH / that wer presente / And with a
grete Astonyynge aH hertys were smyten / this woman, acceptable
to God, norysshyd forth this calf berynge yn hymselfe opyn toknys
of the heuenly marke / And yn due tyme browght with her / the
calf to the Chirche of the Apostle, and fulfillid her vowe, blessynge
God / that makith grete / And vnsercheable thyng*is* with-owte
numbre / whoes grete / vertu and wysdome is with-owte numbre.

¶ CAP*ITULU*M 7^{m.}

¶ A grete myracle of a fragment of brede.

CErteyne shypmen at sandwyche, glad and mery / with a
prosperous cowrse forowid the dowtable see.[2] And them
askyng the depth of the see / that / that / was beforne
y-pesid / now was excitid by þe rage of wyndys; And the for-
warners of variaunte tempeste to come / the clowdys yn heuyn,
ranne a-bowte. the swellynge [sea],[3] yn his feruor with the hepys
growyng of wawys / leift vp hym-self. And cast the shippe nowe
hydyr / now thydyr / the gouerner wyste neuer whydyr to come /
whydyr he shulde turne hym / yn that / that the gretenes of peryH
hadde stonyid ther * mynde / berefte them discrecyoun of ther crafte   *[f. 65 v.]
/ the wawys smyte vppon them, And more myghtly caste them
in-to the wawys / thane bare them vp, and the vnhappy shypmen
thus owte of the wey y-caste. At the laste they were drownd /
oone of them oonly cleuyd to the flittynge maste / and with aH
his myghtys / ascendid on the tree / and saate a-boue. Whiche,
ther sittynge and sumwhat commynge to hymself / to the erys of
Godis[4] / he sesid nat to crye. and askid the blessid Apostle of
Cryist, seynt Barthilmew, to be nygh hym / that sumwyse he
myght this peryH askape / And whan he longe hadde y-multiplied
his prayer / And no remedye sawe commynge neir / he seid / " O
glorious Apostle of Criste, Barthilmewe / how ofte haue I callid
the / in the Article of so grete nede / And I haue nat deseruyd

---

[1] profunda dei.   [2] dubia sulcabant equora.
[3] *Omitted in* M.S. (*In Latin*, mare tumidum.)   [4] divine pietatis.

to be graciously I-herde / therfore ther is no thynge els nowe to me but deithe / .I. beseke the, At the mercy of God / be meyn for my synnys, that I, that haue not deseruyd to be delyuered from these perellys / lette nat me be deputid to euerlastyng flammys / that whatsumeuer yn this presente lyf be denayid me of mercy may be fulfillid yn tyme to come / by thyn interuencioun and merytys." To hym thus seyynge, beholde Anoone was present the glorious Apostle of God / with gladsum face and plesaunte chere / And at his beke or wyll the ire of wyndys were restreynyd / the feruor of the swellyng see was I-sesid / clerenes to heuyn / tranquyllite to the see was I-3euen / he, beyng nygh to the criynge man, seyid / "thy wepyng sighys of thyn contrite herte sownyd yn-to myne erys / ne I. denayid nat to 3eue the helpe / but delayd hit / nowe, therfore, come .I. to the, a mes*sanger of good tydyngis / to 3eue the a 3eifte of desirid helth / for why. the mercyfull lorde hath pardonyd thy lyif. And loo, a shippe of Douyr shall come to the, and receyue the / and glad and hole restore the to thy frendys" / He, thus seyynge, porrectid to hym A pece of breid / And yn a moment vanysshid away / from his sight. An anoone a Shippe of Douyr was presente, In the whiche he was receyuyd aftir the worde of Apostle / hole and glad come home to his / And than tho thyngys, the whiche the pite of glorious Apostle Anenst hym magnyficently hadde .I.-shewid: with feithfull relacyoun he made opyne / And to the confirmacion of the heuenly benefeit / the part of breid that the Apostle 3aue hym he shewid / magnifiynge God, whiche puttyth a terme to the see / whiche all thynge / whatsumeuer he will he doith.

* [f. 66]

¶ CAPITULUM. 8ᵐ.

¶ Also a myracle y-donne yn the see.

AN nothir tyme befill a-nothir myracle / marchauntys of flawndrys with chargid vessellys. with marchaundise / hauynge wynde and wedir, enterid the see, dredyng noon aduersyte / and, faueryng the see / purposid to Lundone / And whan they were passyng by the myddys of the see / Loo, here gladnes was turnyd yn-to waylyng / and ioye in-to sorowe / Lyif yn-to deith; vnwarys brake vp an violent tempest, And, swellyng

the wawys / of the see / with vnhappy fortune the last happe of
vnfortune was trowid nygh to them / What shall .I. drawe my
sermon a-longe / the wyndis contynually wexynge woyde / boith
shippe & shipmen were cast in-to the depthe of the see / And both
the shippe of her marchauntyse And they of ther lyif ar pr*i*uatid
Oone of them only leuyng / to the maste yn the * same .ii. dayes   * [f. 66 v.]
myghtly cleuynge, gret peyne sufferyd ; And yn meyn while he
vsyng the benefete of his voice, he pr*a*yid the vndefawtyng me*r*cy
of criyst, by the merytys of seynt Barthilmewe, myght be neir hym
yn that highest angwyse / to whom, whan for defawtynge of his
hert / the vtteryng of his voice begane to breke / beholde, aforne
the weylyng man seynt Barthilmewe stoid, cherefully confortynge
hym / puttyng forth his hande / And drewe hym owte of the
wawys, and with drye stappys / sette hym at Dykysmuth porte
And so disparisshid / And he, fre from all peryll, was not vnkende
to the ve*r*tu and grace of the Apostle / but what he hadde
sufferid of greyf / what of mercy he hadde optenyd / by the
holy Apostle / with trewe worde he made hit opyne / ȝeuynge
thankys to God. In whom who that trustith / ys nat con-
fowndid / and who that callith hym in-to hymself is not
cotempnyd.

CAPITULUM. 9ᵐ.

Of a yonge man*e*, Robert by name.

A Certeyn*e* yonge [man] cumly of person*e*, Robert by name /
from his yonge age norysshid yn courte, from North-
amptone[1] purposid to London*e* / And it happid hym /
thorow a thyke woode to make his passage / where he, wery of his
iorney / toke his reste / on*e* the grownd, and a while with a litill
slepe recreate hym / that, his way begon*e* / the swyfterly he
myght parforme / but loo, whyle he sowghte reest / he fownde
labur, and whan he wolde with a litill reest his wery lymys
refresshe, he was yntanglyd with the snarys of his ennemy. In his
slepe he was raueshid from his resonable wyttys ; In his slepe his
olde ennemy apperid to hym / yn the forme of a right fair woman*e* /
the whiche with flateryng chere it semyd. to haue sitte at his hede ;

---

[1] It is curious that the passport in the Rules and Orders is made out for a native of Northampton.

And whan, with flaterynge blandysh / A goodwhyle she * hadde flateryd hym / And smothid hym / she put a litiłł bird yn to his moweth, And so apperid no more / the man, awakid. was afrayed of this vnwount vision / and the same houre he lost his wytte / and resoun of all myght was priuate[1] / and what was for to be done / or lefte, he knew nat / ledynge hym woidenes[2] / nowe this way / now that way / he wanderid rennynge / vnknowynge what he did / hastyly he went whedyr the ympetuousnes of the malicious woodenes ympellid hym // At the last he was takyne at Lundone, And browght to the Chirche of seynt Barthilmewes / And ther yn shorte space his witte was recoueryd; where a litiłł tyme he taried / blessyng God, þat to his Apostles hath vouchesaf to commytte his excellent power / to hele syke / to clense lepers / and to caste owte feendys.

¶ CAPITULUM. 10ᵐ.

Of a certeyne knyght, Radulph[3] by name.

A Certeyne knyght, Rayf by name / of the howseholde of William Demunfychet[4] / whan he made his wey by Essex to Londone / by the dome of God[5] / he was rauashid of a feende, and made woid.[6] and yn-to a reprouable witte / be-taken / and he, so woid I-made, slyde downe from his hors / ant rent his clothis / the money that he bar' he skaterid a-brode / and thrywh stonys to them / that he mette with / And now erryng yn wodis / nowe yn hillys / And now a-monge he medyllyd hym self. Amonge the preysse of peple, and them that came aȝenst hym, he cast them yn peryłł or yn drede. Thys mane one a tyme / thowh gretely he withstode / was take / And browght to the same Chirche / and whan he hadde taryed ther .ii. nyghtys, he come to his mynde again).

---

[1] deprived.   [2] madness.
[3] The title of this chapter in the Latin life is "De milite quodam Willelmo nomine," but it goes on "Miles quidam Radulphus nomine de familia Willelmi de Munfichet."
[4] The family of Montfichet flourished in England from 1066 to 1258, and the name is still preserved at Stansted Mountfitchet, in Essex. There were two Williams of the name. The first founded the abbey of Stratford Langton, in 1135, and was not living in Henry II.'s reign; the second, his nephew, is a witness of the charter of foundation of that abbey, and is probably the lord whose retainer Rayf was.
[5] judicio Dei.   [6] mad.

¶ CAPITULUM. 11ᵐ.

Of a certeyne mannys sone.

Ther' was also in the Towne / of Berwyk¹ a certeyn man / *Spylmane by name / that vsid the plowe / And solde woode / And with woode to sylle / he come to Londone. y-know to many men, he hadde a childe that was greuously syke
5 with the fallynge evill / the fallynge evill, aftir phisiciens, is a syknes / that compressith the ventriclis and the weys of the brayne / lettyng the operacion of the wyttis / as sight, heryng, and othir bodyly wyttys takith a-way, and werith all the body with an harde passioun / this childe, laborynge yn² this sykenes / was
10 browght to the forsaid chirche / yn the solempnyte of the glorious Apostle / and whan the .iiij. lessoun of his passioun was redde / the helth receyuyd of all his membris / he come to kysse the auctur / And than, nat a litill, he accendid yn to deuocioun / all that wer ther presente to the Laude of God / and the blessid Apostle / and
15 nat oonly of the comyn pepyll, but also of the clergye / thankynges were ʒeue to God / for why he ys good / & forwhy in-to the worlde. his mercy is.

*[f. 67 v.]

CAPITULUM. 12ᵐ.

Of the doughtyr of wymunde the preyst.

A Preiste, Wymunde by name / that gouernyd the Chirche of seynt Martyn³ that is situate yn the corner of the wey /
20 that ledith to Westmynster, many yeres he had receyuyd one hym, by the institucyoun of the bysshoppe of Londone / the deynrye of nygh chirches for maters ecclesiasticall to discusse. This man, byʒonde equyte ʒeuen to voluptuous lyif / and his incontinence / was euer redy to slyde to the worse / nat refreyn-
25 ynge / with the bridill of clennes and chastite / Purchasid hym a

---

¹ The Latin MS. gives the true name of this town *Bernech*, Barnack, in Northamptonshire.
² yn *is repeated in the MS*.
³ St. Martins in the Fields. This is probably the Wymund, "dean of Lincoln," recorded as having held the stall of Neasdon in St. Paul's Cathedral. (Le Neve : Fasti. II. 414.) His exact date is unknown, but it was between 1103 and 1162, and may have been near the latter year, so that his daughter might easily be grown up in 1174, the year of these wonders.

lemman / and of her vnlefully begait a doughtir, whome he,
lovynge with fadirly affeccioun / yn yonge age put her to lern-
ynge / And whan she came to age of mariage / put her to a
matrone / the whiche yn a wommannys breyste hadde a mann*ys
herte / and refreynyd her from that vice that folowyth that age / 5
and with holsumme doctryne studied to enforme her / the mayde,
therfore, was kepte attendawntly, and with chaaste discipline
informyd / and she begane to be wyser than her techer, And for to
shewe the forme and example of virgynal puryte / to all them that
lyued abowt her / Certeyn whan of many wowers / this virgyn was 10
desirid / she myght nat by noon cautelys or suttyll suggestioun be
deceyuyd / for neuer wolde not she admytte the flaterynge speche
of bawdys or lechorys / but the Carnal drawghtis of voluptuosite
she, tamynge, myghtly troid them vndir foit / vnspottid euermore
abidyng. Thys clennes envied the ennemye of man-kynde / 15
wyllynge to subuerte yn her the purpos of clennes. And new
suttelteys of noyyng he consellid and sowghte. And vnherde
deceytys ordeynyd and fownde aȝenst the virgyne / the whiche
sufferynge the rightwysnes of God / not oonly we merveyle / but
also drede / For thowh God ynwardly beholdynge howh it myght 20
be done / we be demynge to vs this a monstruous thynge / Therfore
this suttell serpent, transformyng hym-self. yn-to the lyknes of a
fair yonge man / As he hadde be a gentill-mane of the kyngis
blode, more vylyfycat with precyous ornamentis / than I-bewtified
for shynyng of his bewte / thus sodenly slyde yn-to the Chambyr / 25
where sole this mayde sate / the whiche I-seyne / with a sodayn fray
she was smytte / And whens he came / And howe he entrid, she
was astonyed and meruellid / and behelde the bewty / and the
shynynge of his chere † with a sympyl / but nat with a prudent ye.
the ennemy felt the drede / of the light wommanhede / wherfore he 30
drewe nyghyr, and sate downe by her syde / And owte of mortall
and dedly breste he cast owte harde venym. First trewly
with swete venymys wordis comfortid the dredfull / and than
prayers and promyssis medillid / yn that she wolde grawnte her
assent to fowylle vse / And yn the meyne while / he knytte his 35
engynnys / of sotell deseyt / the mayde a litill withdrewe her
drede, And toke an hardynes of speche / And thus she Answerd:
"It is no prudent mannys dede / that vsith reson / suche a
conseyuyd desire yn herte / so vnshamfully to vttyr / ne so
vnsemely will to do / Firste / it were sittyng the nobiley of thy 40

birthe to shewe to my parentys / And than, *with* consent of vs
bothe / the lawe of matrymony to make / And that .I-contracte.
and streghthyd with solempne Auctorite of the chirche halowynge /
and so to pay the dette of body, eche of vs to othyr, nat for
bernynge luste, but oonly by cause of gen*er*acion. Thou purposist
alweyes the contrary way / thou makyst no mencion of God / nethir
of man / but only purposist the fury and wodenys of thyn voluptuous
soule / And so, the shame of God / and of man y-putte behynde /
thou prayst me to consent to thyn maligne voluptuosyte / Fyrst, forsothe, telle me who and what thou art / and by whom a wyttnes thou
art hydder admyttyd, And of other thyng*is* heer' / aftyr vse thou
bettyr concell, and be bettyr avisid." / To this the ennemy answerid /
"what sekist thou heyr the ordir of reson / wher only we talke to-
gidre for oure wylle? heyr pite is wynnyng¹ / religiou*n* is sup*er*-
sticion * / Where oure dede and purpos ys of the wracke of chastite /   *[f. 69]
no lawe / no custome is to be consellyd / but oonly the rewarde of
vnclennesse is to be attendid / wherfore to aske this / who .I. am
and howh .I. cam hidyr, it is but voyde to enquere / oonly to my
peticion ioyne thyn*e* affeccio*un* / And aftir p*r*omysse, swiftly an
hastly shall folowe effecte." ¶ Aftir theys and moo yn this wyse,
whan they hadde to-gider said / the noryssh² of the virgyn*e*,
cu*m*mynge vppon*e*, mervellid with whom she spake / she herde a
voyce of oone that spake / but she sawh no man / but the mayden /
At whois cu*m*myng, the ennemy disparysshid a-wey / but ȝeit he
was nat forȝeitfull of the vnshamefaste boldnes / wher that eu*er* the
mayde he sawh aloyne / In the man*er* of a wantan, ioly yonge
mane, yn like ordyr he callid on*e* the mayde; she, trewly, with
prayer / and tokyn*e* of the crosse / her-self wardyng, so defendyd /
that for all his engy*n*nys and waytys she skapid vntowchid / On*e*
a day, whan the mayde was sole yn her chambre / this malignynge
theyf was p*r*esente, fayryr than he was woo*n*nt / with shynynge
chere. ¶ And first he yaue prayers, And aftir, promysse / and
whan with this nothyng he p*r*ofitid / he arayed to brynge yn
violence, whois boldnes the virgyne felynge beforn*e* / with grete
cryes she fulfillid the howse / In the meyn whyle / whan*e* the
s*er*uantes raan to the noyse / the malignyng ennemy went his way /
And smytte the virgyne, seyyng / "Why wolt nat thou consente /
and receyue of my ȝyftis? / su*m*what now thow shalt feil / what may

---

¹ pietas questus.   ² nurse.

the hande doo of myn enmyte." And An-noon, yn the goynge
a-way of the ennemy / the virgyne fyll downe yn-to erth / owte of
her wytte / and with * a grete passion / yn her body was tormentid,
And wallowynge ofte / and azene turnyng with ynordynate gesture /
of her lymmys, the sorow wytnesyd deith.¹ To whom rennyng, the
seruantes fownde her halfe a-lyue, And with a compleynynge noyse.
fulfillid the howses. The neyghborys were gaderyd all abowte, and
grete confluence of peple / for the novelte of suche a dede / And all
the peple were turnyd / yn-to A stonyynge / and an horror / And
whan the virgyne was thus longe y-tormentid, At the laste fomynge
at the moweth / aftyr many sighyngis / a litill she toke breith /
And tolde [what] was done abowte here / how the spirite of
malice / hadde aperid / And with what promysse / he hadde
Atemptid / to drawe here to consente of vnclennesse / And howe,
confusid, goynge Away, he smytte her / And aftir the stroke so
greuous, Infirmyte folowid / And vneith she hadde endid her
wordys / And loo, azeen / the same wyse / As be-forne / she begane
to be tormentid / Therfore whan / twyes / or thryes / euery day /
and sumwhyle moerᵉ oftynner, she was so I-tormentid, ¶ By the
peticioun of the same virgyne, & consell of her Parentys / she was
browghte to the ⹁Chirche of seynt Barthilmewe / and she was
borne forth one a Carpete² / And passid forth Aforne the hospitall
of the same; the forsaid ennemy was present / seyynge to the
virgyne / "Whidir art thou borne? trowyst thou that the Apostle
shall delyuer the from myne handys? yf thou graunte nat and
conseynt to me / with lenger and harder dysesys / thou, vexid and
made wery, shall dye." / Azene also, whan she was put downe /
frome the Carpent for to be borne yn-to the chirche, he apperid to
her, seyyng, "Stonde, mayde, stonde! And forbydde † to be borne
yn-to the chirche / for I shall zeue the helth / and all that is
desirable to helth / at thyne wylle I shall make zeuyn / to flowe to
thyne hande." And to this / the mayde answerde no thynge / but
trustid yn God / and, her handys lyfte vp yn-to heuyn / she
besowghte the mercy of God. Therfore this wykkid ennemy,
seynge hymself thus deluded and scorned, with sharper prikkyngis
wexid woide azenste the virgyne / And with a moore greuous
passioun / thane he was wount, smyt her. The chanouns of the

---

¹ inordinato gestu membrorum internum testatur dolorem. Latin MS.,
32 A. col. 1, line 1—3.
² carpet, Latin MS. carpento, a litter.

Chirche was ther present / seyng this / And with deuout prayers besowght the Apostle / that with his woonnte pyte he wolde succur' this laborynge virgyne. ¶ Oure Lorde graciously herde his praynge seruantes / askynge that was right. And by the merytys of
5 the holy Apostle / delyuerid the virgyne from the feende / And so delyuerd / restorid her fully to her helth / the mayde than was betake to her parentys / the whiche, all yn God[1] ioyynge / prechid euerywhere / the vertu of the Apostle / praysyng and blessyng God / the whiche hatyth no thynge that he hath made / whois domys[2]
10 bene manyfolde depe derkenesse.

¶ CAPITULUM. 13ᵐ·

Of a feuerus mane that lackid his ye sight.

Certeyne man of the castell of Chillam[3] take with grete syknes, In sorowe and byttyrnes of herte / lede his vnhappy lyfe / Atte the laste, sorowe grewe vppone sorowe / for his Axses[4] encresynge, he lost the light of boith yen / therfor he
15 graspid abowte / trustynge to othir mennys paysse / and sayynge his way. with his stayff / and so a certeyn tyme he sate yn derknes / Now the .ix.ᵗʰᵉ monyth was passid / whan the wrecch cessid nat of his contynuall syknes / euer cryynge * and askynge, and askyng and criynge, tyll the mercy of God wolde here hym.   * [f. 70 v.]
20   ¶ Whan he come, trewly, to the chirche of seynt Barthylmewe the holy Apostle / he receyuyd light of boith yene / and for the gyfte opteynyd, he, ȝyldynge thankys to God / boith to lerned and othir that stode Abowte, witnessid feithfully / the vertu of cryistis Apostle.

CAPITULUM. 14ᵐ·

¶ Of a certeyne yonge man y-bownde.

25   Certeyne yonge mane takyne of his ennemyes y-bownde / was borne yn a Carte / for to be commyttyd to a streyter warde. ¶ And whan the passage was made by the same chirche / yn goynge / he callid vppone the name of the holy

---

[1] Latin MS., *in domino*.   [2] *judicia*.
[3] Chilham castle, six miles from Canterbury, includes parts of a Norman keep which was standing in the time of this man.   [4] *febre*.

Apostle / And sodenly he fownde hym-self I-losid / And An-noon he skippid owte of the Carte and enteryd the chirche. ¶ And yn this wyse he skapid / the handis of his ennemyes.

CAP*ITULU*M. 15ᵐ·

¶ Of a certeyn yonge mane dum.

A Certeyne yonge man / while haply he lay grouelynge one the grownde / desirynge Awhile to rest hym-self / by the 5 malice of the olde ennemye / he wexed dumme / And so, lakkynge his speche, of a certeyne yonge womane, cosyn to hym / was leid and browgħt to the same chirche. ¶ And boitħ of them knelid downe a-fore the holy Auter. And witħ waylyng hertys besowgħte the helpe of seynt Barthilmewe / And the same day / 10 was restorid to hym / the office of his tonge.

CAP*ITULU*M. 16ᵐ· [and 17ᵐ·]

Of a marchaunte.

*[f. 71]

THer came one a day to the sayd chirche a certeyn mane / And askid to speke witħ the bretheryn / And what that happid to hym / he wolde exp*r*esse / he was browgħte yn to the Chapter howse / And the chanou*n*s beyng p*r*esente / thus he began 15 to speke ¶ "That ye may knowe / howħ pituous and * howe glorious A patrou*n* ye haue / her, my lordis / what late happid to me / And to my felshippe / and consider that he that ye worshipe yn ertħe / yn heuyn and yn the see / is of grete mercy / and of grete vertu. ¶ We were yn A Shippe / many of vs to-gider / And 20 Arysynge vp a sodayn tempest, we began to perysshe / yn so mykiħ that, mystrustynge to leue / oonly we abyded the last houre of oure periħ / In the meyne whyle / we cessid nat to wayle for oure synnys / to knocke oure brystys / to calle yn-to vs many helpys of seynt*is* / and trewly, yn the hyndyr part of the Shippe / 25 witħ tremulynge lippys / And sorowfuħ hert, y besowghte the mercy of God / where I. herde a voyce, seyyng / 'what crye ȝe vpone so many namys of seynt*is*? And youre Patrou*n* by specyal p*r*iuylege / grawntid of God / to yow / ȝe lacches to calle.' To

whom I seyed, 'who is that, my lord?' / And he seid / 'most
blessid Barthilmew calle ye yn-to you / And hym ȝe shaH feiH
most prompte helper In this present periH.' And forthwith / I
cam to my felshippe / And tellid what I herde / And that they
shulde yeue feith / ther-to / yn aH wyse I monyschid them.
¶ And than to-gidyr, with one soule, and inwarde affeccioun of
hert / with grete clamoure of voice / we callid yn the holy Apostle
to ȝeue his helpe / to wrecchis perysshynge / and to graunte vs
port salfe, seyynge / 'Lord / Lord / saue vs / we perysch; oure
helth ys yn thyn hande / lette thy mercy loke vppone vs / And
securly we shaH serue the' / O mervellous is to sey / to the aȝeyne-
criynge / of that holy name, the elementys yeue way to vs / and
seruyd oure wille / The Sky, that beforne was derke, clothid hym
yn hys light / the see cesid from his feruor / the trowblys tempestuous wyndis vttirly rested them. *And so forth than aftyr brethynge   *[f. 71 v.]
of softe plesaunte wynde / that ys callid ȝephirus / we saylid. and
optenyd a port / And nowe we came to the chirche of oure
delyuerer / And for the benefeit y-govyn to vs of so grete a pite,
both to hym and to you, the seruantys and frendys of hym / we
ȝeue thankynge, and to God; O ye happy. And weylsum / ȝe /
and most weylsum religious men / that ioye her vndyr so clere a
duke / so myghty a prince / And so mercyfuH A fadir! Of vs ye
may considre / how muche ȝe may trust and hope of hym / of
consolacioun and of grace / for whyle he was so mercyfuH to vs /
so strange from his[1] seruyce / what benygnyte And how muche
reseruyth he / to his most belouyd seruantys" / thus he seyid /
And commendynge hym-self. to the prayers of the bretheryn / he
offerid his oblacion / and ioynge from ioyfulmen / he toke his way.

CAPITULUM. 18ᵐ·

¶ Of a certeyne marchaunte.

IN that tyme that [Henry] the secunde, kynge[2] of Englond,
besegid Walys / with strange hande[3] / it happid A notable
myracle / And worthy to be tolde / Ther was a man of
Colchester / hauyng oportunyte to exsecute that he had decreid /

---

[1] MS. *repeats* his.
[2] The Latin reads: *Henricus secundus rex anglie.* Henry II. invaded Wales in 1157. Matthew Paris, Rolls ed., II., 214.
[3] cum valida manu.

yn his mynde / that were nedefull to the hoyste lyynge at that seygge. Of his goodis he studied to bryng thidir / and that he wolde be solde / he sette yt at a price as he wolde, And with-yn shorte tyme wan̄ muche money. ¶ And whan he hadde layid it vppe diligently / In certeyn⸴ the seyid mane had sum penyes, the 5 whiche of a vowe / were dettefull to the Chirche of seynt Barthylmewe / Neuertheles he reteynyd these / that these with othir of his owne / by ofte eschangynge he wolde had multiplied / And *yn oportune tyme bothe his vowe / And whatsumeuer encressid a-boue / of his vowe / he wolde brynge hyt to the forsaid chirche / 10 therfore whan he disposid hym-self to turne home to his / And be watyr he was coartid¹ to make his passage / the shippe with othir, no thynge demynge of evyl / he enterid / And whan they saylid forth / he slepyd / his money layid / vndir his hede / In the meyn whyle / oone that wente with hym conceyuyd hit, And he 15 ouercummen with desire of that money / theyfly withdrew hyt / And whan they cam to the port, vndyr a certeyne stone / nat fer from the port / he hidde hit / the mane Awakid, sowg̃hte his money And fownde it nat / Inquyryd of hys felshipe / yf ony mane yn game or ernest had take hyt / they for his demawndynge 20 ȝeif hym rebukys / hauynge scorne that he shulde reprove them of theyft, the whiche feith̄full felshipe he hadde / Therfore, wher' he saw that mannys helpe was vttirly denayd hym / with all his soule he conuertid hym-self to God, and with an ynward waylynge / shedynge owte for sorowe terys / cessid nat to calle one the mercy 25 of the blessid Apostle Barthylmewe / And loo, in the sylence of the derke nygh̄te / to hym slepynge Apperid yn a visioun / the glorious Apostle of God / And in thys maner many thyngis with hym he talkid / "O," he said, "mane / what cryiste thou soo oncessantly, and with Importune cryes cessist nat to vnreste me?" 30 / And he sayd / "thou knowist, and well knowist, syr' / the cause of my crye / and it is no nede to opyne to the / the maner of my wrecchidnesse / the whiche so many sigh̄yngys yn wepynge and waylyng I haue opynd A-forne thy face / and ageyne reherssid hyt / no, it † is not hidde from thy pite, from how grete Ioye / In-to 35 how grete waylyng / from howe grete ricches / with sodeyne case / I am come yn nedynes / and of so grete an hurte / ther is to me no remedy / ne no cownsell ȝevyne. Therfore the Allone I trustid

---

¹ Et per aquam transire necessitas itineris cogeret.

/ that my solace shulde come / Thou therfore / that thou mayist ȝoe and for thou mayste / helpe me / hauyng mercy of me" / To whom answered the seynt / " This money for whoes lost / thus thou lamentyst / vnriȝhtwysly thou hast gotyne / And whyle .
5 with myne helpe, thou askyst to be of that restorid / so thou askist that thou woldyst make me partyner of thyn synne / the whiche of the riȝhtwys dome of God / thou hast lost; And for cause, yn rycchynge of thy-self / othir men thou spoylid vndredfully / now thou begynnyst to nede / and othir haue and consume
10 thy rycches ¶ ȝe, forsothe, marchauntis / men of vntrew soule / forsakers of trewth and equite / nat dredynge God / ne hauynge compassioun of youre euyn crystene[1] / with gyle and othys al men bygilynge / ye presente God and his seyntes / wytnes to youre wyckednes / consumynge othir mennys poochys to fulfill your
15 pursys // who, therfore, shulde haue mercy one yowe ? / who shulde norysshe suche wrecchis / nat mercyable yn so grete A malice ? " / " Lord," he seyide, " yf .I. haue vnriȝhtwysly gete my money / ȝit sum of that I haue decreid / to conuerte yn-to goode werkys, And with them to visite thy chirche / And purpose to
20 rewarde thy seruantys ther" / " O," seid he / " this is your woodnes / that whan, with many wylys / ȝe haue spoylyd pore men / that of the raueyn of pore men / sumwhat to the worshipe of God ye depart / that more securly ye may abyde yn youre synne / and yn thys * wyse ȝe trowe to pees God / but God hatyth raueyne ȝeuen
25 yn-to sacryfyce / And no more the ȝiftis of suche men plesith hym / than the wagis of strompethode, Or the sacrifice of an hownde / or as he that wolde sacrifice the childe to the fadyr / Neuertheles, wher-of ioyest thou, telle me / And whan thou visitid my chirch." " I wolde," he seyid, " and purposid / but with dyuers
30 bysynes I-lette, .I. myȝht nat come thidyr" / And than the seynt Answerid / " Whan all thyng habowndid with the / thou haddist no tyme. to come to my chirche / to prayse God / to redeme thy synnys / now, y-sped and delyueryd of all / thou hast noon impediment / ne no perell of drede / surely whidir that euer thou
35 wolt / thou mayst goo" / And he seyid / " Lord / how may .I. presume thy glorious temple to aske or desire / and, voyde from sacrifice / in the siȝht of God and of the to appere?" " Nay," sayid he, ".I. nede nat thy ȝiftis / It is sufficient to me y-nowh

* [f. 73]

---

[1] nec proximis compacientes.

the grace of God / for to prouyde for the nede of my clerkis / ne
.I. am nat vnmyghty to ȝeue fode to them / that seruyth me" /
"That ys trowth," seyed the merchawnt / "therfore, my goode
lorde / leste hapley my wykydnes be more than thy copyous
goodnys / Loo, heyr before the / of my trespace .I. repente ; be- 5
hestyng amendis. That the mony whiche sumtyme .I. promysid /
to thy chirche / And more .I. avowe me thedir to brynge." To
this the Apostle answeryd / "And .I." seyid he / "vndir this
condicioun, trewly shall not dyscouer the gilty by name / but to
hym of whom thy money shulde dewly be asked ageyne, .I. shall 10
gyf cownsell / to seye / that he of thy felshipe late skunfitid in
batayll / priuely toke a-way thy money / and yn to thys tyme
hath kepte hyt hole / and .I. of this nat vnknowynge / haue not
y-sufferid hym to * lessen hit / In that I knewe beforne that thou
callidist vpone me / that by me / thou myghtstid thy loosse 15
recouere." At theys wordys, speche and visioun made an ende.
The mane awakid / that he sawh and herde besyly reuoluyd yn
his mynde / discussynge diligently / the lyfe and dede of his
felshippe / And by hym-self no thyng certeyn myght comprehende
/ At the laste he ȝaue way to a flittyng and a tempestuous varyaunte 20
soule / and began to aske and cownsell a preyst I-lernyd by
scripture yn suche visions / what were goode yn thys to be donne.
And the preyste cownsellid, dowtys layid a-parte / and commawndid hym to ȝeue feith / to that he herde / seyynge hit were
impossible / to be othir wyse / than the Apostle hadde sayde / It 25
plesid, therfore / them bothe to calle oone of the kyngis mynystris,
for þat to such men dyuers thyngis ben knowe that ben doyn in
many placys / þe which ofte bene present yn pleys, in quarellys,
in sclawndrys, In Iugementis / þerfor þei went to-gidir to þe
provost of þat place / & with promyssys prayed him to be 30
fauorable to þes beforsaid / And so þey declarid to him al þe
processe of this mater. And by the dylygence of this man / the
man was sowght and fownde / And browght yn-to a secrete place /
And, only presente the provost and the doer of the trespace / he
was callid yn of the preyste, and opposid / And the preyste prayd 35
hym / and exhortid hym / that he wolde restore the money / that
he toke a-way, vndyr the mannys hede / whan he slepid / And
this he seyed ; "I was shewid and ynformyd, veryly, with so trew
a wytnesse / the whiche, by commyne estymacioun, myght nat
lye" / therfore, yf he wolde ynclyne / to ther cownsellys, he may 40

go vnhurte / yf he wolle denay hit / the kyng*is* officer / hym as a
theyf may * holde / and sesyn*e* / And for to be condempnyd / be-   * [f. 74]
take hym to the Iugys. / He Anoone fuH of drede / drewe the
preist a-parte / and his gilt confessid / restorid to hym the money
5 yn hole su*m*me / and no harme sufferynge, frely went his way /
By this maner the forsaid man*e* by seynt Barthylmewe receyuyd /
that was take from hym / And aftirward, co*m*myng to his chirche
/ offerid that he vowid / And to the bretheryn of the place / aH
thyng that was do*n*ne abowte hym opynly declaryd.

¶ CAP*ITU*LUM 19ᵐ·

¶ Of a certeyn*e* yonge woman.

10   A Certeyn*e* yonge woman*e* was yn the Cyte of London*e* I-
know to many men / And as an hyryd seru*a*nt / wounte
to serue many men / the more was know*e* / thys. woma*w*),
one a day / by a bawde bigilid / from the profite of her iust
laboure / to voluptuousnes of vncleyne synne / & by the robber of
15 her clennesse, wylfully admyttynge, she was robbid of yncomperable
tresu*r*e / Ne it was nat longe / but Loo, the reward of syne folowid
/ and where her hole body and fleyssh she made sugget to synne /
vttirly she lost her hole mynde / and that membris that were
armo*u*re of wykkidnes / be turnyd yn-to Armur' of woodnesse. the
20 hert that is pryncipaH of man / *with* opp*re*ssiou*n* of the feende /
the whiche was onyd to hym / was derkid / And that which yn
syn*e* / God wolde nat drede / In peyn*e* / nethir God / ne hym-
self vndirstode / the yen*e* now left vp a*n*) hye / now dredfully
rollid abowte / her clothis be-rente with her handys / the tonge was
25 vnbridillid to blasfemy / and rybawdy / And, encresynge her   † [f. 74 v.]
woodenes, y-streyned she was yn streyghte bondys / these † bondys
with her woodnys myght / lightly y-broke / othir were addid ther-
to / thus she was brought to the hospitale of the seyid chirche /
and yn short tyme folowid contraxiou*n* of aH membris / that yn no
30 wyse myght she vse them frely / And yn so grete a wrecchidn*e*s /
was p*re*sente the mercy of the blessid Apostle / the whiche the
madde woman*e* losid of her woodnes me*r*cyfully / and erectid the
contracte¹ myghtly / and fulhole went home to her owne.

¹ *the contr*a*cte*, cripple.

CAPITULUM. 20ᵐ·
Of a woman y-take with the palsy.

AN nothir womman dyssoluyd with the palsy / and growynge ynwardly . the greuous syknes, sufferid throwys of all her membrys / she dwellid vppone Temse¹ And to the same howse she was browght; and þe same woman, with the vertu of the Apostle / aftir a litill tyme was curid of her syknes, and ioynge, wente home to her howse / toke an howsbond, and browght forth childryne.

CAPITULU . 21ᵐ·
A myracle of a mayde.

A Certeyn mayde and seruant of a cytyseyne of Londone was browghte to the forsaid hospitalle / the whiche myght nat strecche forth ony fote / that she hadde / or for longe syknes y-vexid / she hadde kepte her bedde longe / or by-cause her synewys of hammys were contract. The blessid Apostle, one a nyght, apperid to her yn her slepe / commaundid her to strecche owte her feite / and she, at the commawndment of the Apostle / lightly her foit did owte strecche / and yn the mornyng risynge vp, she hadde helth of the toone / and at evensong tyme she hadde fre vse of both / they mervelid that were presente / And askid her what betidid her that nyght / And she tolde / what she sawh / And confessid the * auctor of her helth / praysynge the Apostle of cryist, and ȝeuyng thankyngis to God.

[f. 75]

¶ CAPITULUM 22ᵐ·
¶ Also a myracle of a certeyne woman.

THe yeir of incarnacioun of oure Lord. M.C.² and Lᵗⁱ and nyne / of the reigne of kynge Richard the secunde / the sixtene / In the solempnyte of the Apostle seynt Barthilmewe / many

---

¹ *Temse*, Thames.
² The Latin reads : *Millesimo centesimo quinquagesimo nono regni Henrici secundi regis sexto decimo.* *Quinquagesimo* is an error for *sexagesimo.* The sixteenth of Henry II., who is the king meant, was 1169—70 ; but it is clear that the writer was not very exact in the use of the regnal year, for Stephen died October 25, 1154, and Henry was crowned December 19, 1154, so that by calculating from either the feast of St. Bartholomew (August 24) 1169 is in the fifteenth and not in the sixteenth year of Henry II.

tokynnes of vertu were shewyd yn his holy chirche / A certeyn
wommane laborynge yn greuous sykenes / that was borne yn an
horslytter / to that holy temple / And beholde, yn the vigill of the
same Apostle / Abowte the houre of complyne / she begane bettir
5 to haue / And a litill, her myghtys that she hadde lost she
resumyd / and forthermore, anoone aftir, ful helth optenyd; For
why ioynge and hole, she rooys owte of her lyttyr / And come to
kys the hye Auter / offerynge her-self yn-to an acceptable hoist to
God / with grace and thankis yeldynge / Anooyn the godly myracle
10 was made opyne And of the conuent of that chirche / and mykil
peple, praysyng and thanke was ȝeue to God / deuoutly / And to
his blessid Apostle.

¶ CAP*ITULU*M 23ᵐ.¹

¶ Of a childe that receyuyd his syght.

IN the same solempnyte / a certeyne childe / that hadde lost
hys sight / by the meyn of the holy Apostle receyuyd hit
15 ageyne / And he, seynge with othir seers the mercy of God /
and the vertu of the blessid Apostle seynt Barthymewe / with
the shewyng of the heuynly tokyne gretly he magnyfied and
prechid.

¶ CAP*ITULU*M 24ᵐ.

Of a wommane that hadde lost her oone syde.

IN the same chirche, yn the forsayd solempnyte / a certeyne
20 woman was browght / the whiche one * a tyme / slepynge one   * [f. 75 v.]
the toone side / was smyte with a Palsy / And lost that
side² / And yn that destitucyoun of her lymmys / duryd nat a litill
tyme. This womman, yn the nyght of the holy solempnyte was
helid / And with ioye, hole went home / to her owne.

¹ The number of each chapter is written in the margin of the manuscript
in red. In this place, and in most, Capᵐ. 23ᵐ ; in some places, Caplm. Arabic
numerals are used, and the Roman numerals of this text are to be taken as
representing the Latin word indicated by the Arabic numeral and the contraction above it. The Latin version has no numbers to the chapters.
² Que quodam tempore dormiens uno latere paralisi percussa est: unum
latus amiserat.

CAP*ITULU*M 25ᵐ.

Of a litill childe that was madde.

Aftir the vtas[1] / of the same feiste / A certeyne litiłł childe was browgħt of his modyr to that chirche / the whiche, from the feist of seynt Lawrence the martyr / hadde lost ałł felynge of resone / And for his woodnes laborid sore / greuous and intollerable to the modir he was / And as she seid / he was bore by many placys of seyntis a-forne that tyme / but neuer optenyd remedy / And whane his modyr hadde browgħt hym to the forsayd place / And ther hadde fulfillid holy wacche and prayer' / she deseruyd of the most mekest crystys Apostle / the effecte of her peticioun / and so optenyd to her-self gladnes / And to the childe heltħ / and euery sonday folowyng, shewid hym to ałł the peple.

CAP*ITULU*M 26ᵐ.

Of a certeyne womman.

A Certeyn womane of Wyndesouer,[2] / hauynge many beystys, sufferid a grete harme and losse of them by sodeyne deitħ / onely oo cow she hadde a-lyue / remaynyng of that pestilence / And she, lackynge foode / almost was browgħt to the detħ. her neygħborys abowte her / hauynge compassioun of her / and of her sorowys / ȝaue her cownsełł that she shulde beseke the mercy / of the blessid Apostle for this harmys / And make to hym sum promysse, that he wolde restore her' cow, by hys myghty power, that begane to dye / she, yeuynge grete cre*dence to holsome cownsełł / Anoone began to mesure her cowe / that she mygħt haue the mesure / for a ligħt to ben offeryd / of that lengitħ, and so here vow to be parformyd / And a mervelous thynge! Annoon the cowe reuyuyd / and began to ete / As noone harme hadde happid her / In dew tyme the womman came to the forsayid chirche / to ȝelde thankyngis to God / And to his glorious Apostle, And offerid the ligħt that she Avowid / And expressid the benefite of pite / that so mercyfully she hadde receyuyd.

---

[1] Octave. The Latin reads: post octavas ejusdem festivitatis.
[2] *Wyndesover*, Windsor: in the Latin, *de Windlesores*.

¶ CAP*IT*ULU*M* 27ᵐ.

Of the repercioun & fyndynge of an hors.

A Certeyn preist of Kente, co*m*mynge neyr the gladnesse of the feist glorious / pu*r*posid to come to the oftesayid[1] chirche / sittynge on*e* a goode hors / the whiche was deyr to hym / wit*h* othir men / that intendid to the same place / And
5 whan the sonne wente almost to rest / and nyg*h*t derke sprede on the erthe / nede compellid them to take ther yn[2] / And whan they lokid abowte on*e* eue*r*y side / and sye noon hostrye / whydyr they myg*h*te drawe / It plesid them to late ther hors to pasture / And they kepte wacche yn kepynge of ther horssys yn the same place /
10 this y-done / the prestis hors. brake further / noone of them considerynge / nethir the p*r*eist fast a-slepe wyttynge. But what myg*h*te falle / to them of adue*r*site / that hastid wit*h* a desire / to that place of vnwastid pite ? / as who seit*h* noon: euyn by the slepynge preiste A certeyn mane Apperid / hauyng A shynynge
15 chere / and shooke the vestment that he weyr softly, And seyid / "A-rise! why art thou so longe oppressid wit*h* slu*m*mrynge?" / And he, wit*h* a liti*ll* noyse awakid,* risid vp, and lokid this way /   * [f. 76 v.] And that way / And p*a*rsayuyd nat hys hors / neir abowte hym / And whan sorowfully he hadde ranne abowte / And did a*ll* his
20 diligence to seke his hors / he herde the nehyng of his hors / too furowlonges from hym / as he myg*h*te parceyue wit*h* opyne eere. And Annoyn wit*h* his felshippe he folowid / and that he sowg*h*te, he fownde / and skippid on*e* hym / And whane he was co*m*myn to the place desirid / aforne the ymage of the Apostle he fi*ll*
25 p*r*ostrate / And ȝaue thankyng*is* for fyndyng of his hors / And wittnessid that the ymage þ*at* he saw*h* was most like to hym þ*at* waked hym, no thing doughtyng yn hym-self / but that was the Apostle of cryste / that so benyngly hadde directid his way / And his hors, that so deliciously he louyd / and so negligently hadde
30 lost / myg*h*tly hadde restoryd.

[1] ad sepedictam tendebat ecclesiam.   [2] inn.

CAPITULUM 28m.

¶ Of an howse vntouchid yn myddyl of the fyer.

Ho suffisid to opyne expressly / aH the benefetys of the vnwastid pite / that men be wount to telle / that hath be done yn the portys of the see / by the holsome meritys of the blessid Apostle seynt Bartholomewe, vnsessyngly / Of the whiche I haue herde many of them / but for the prolixite of this tretyse / And the symylytude of myracles, .I. haue omysid to write. Therfore they that be brennynge yn his only loue, and vsualy be feruent yn his seruyce to his Chirche / or els to his relikys / brynge ther oblaciouns, And certeynly sumwhat that commyth of wynnyng of ther shippys frely they brynge, kyndely, and ioyfully. Nat only mene but wommen / that bene deuoute abowte his seruyce and worshippe / han bene refresshid with his ofte consolacioun / And be expert / that he is nygh* to them / that callith vppone hym yn treweth / And therfore it is that many of them yerely / with lightis and oblaciouns, peesfuH vowys and prayers, visite hys holy chirche / And be glad to telle of his holy myracles / that haue be done Abowte them / The whiche, syth it is harde aH to expresse / neuertheles oone by grace of example I shall knytte[1] to the forseyed / of the whiche ther be so many wyttnes almost / as ther be men dwellyng yn the porte of Hastynge. ¶ It fiH vpone a tyme / or els be vnwarnes of men / or more by the vengeawnce of God / the Towne callid Hastynge began with woodnesse of fyer to perisshe / There was ther a worshipfuH matrone / Ceale[2] by name / whois howsbonde was callid Helys, a mane commynge home frome be-ʒoonde the see with his shippe, chargid with wyne And applied at Londone / And the same day, vnknowynge the hurte at home, he visitted the Chirche of the holy Apostle / And for hym-self and for aH that partenyd to hym, meke prayers he offerid vp to God / And to the holy Apostle / The forsaid womman, whan she sawh the flammys of fyer drawynge neir to her howse / vtterly vnexpert of mannys cownseH and helpe / with fuH feith / yaue her-self to the suffragyes of seynt Barthylmewe / the blessid Apostle / callynge one hym bisily with ynwarde herte / and deuoutly ofte callynge with-yn her, hys glorious name

---

[1] exempli gracia subnectam.
[2] In the Latin : Cecilia nomine : cujus vir Helyas.

rehersyng, and duplynge prayers / so made a vowe of ligħt to be browgħte to his chirche yn-to his honoure. And she begane Annoyne witħ a longe threid to compasse the howse / and leyfte hit ther fixed / And loo! A mervelous thynge to seye / and beforne
5 dayes vnherde / the fyer ferid the feitħ of the womman / And one euery parte bernyd / And aɫɫ thyng * turnyd yn-to Asshis / And nat presumyd to touche the threid / but flow ouer to the nexte howsys / the howse that was mesurid witħ the threid, hit mygħt nat hurte. Ʒeit abydytħ that mervelous and glorious myracle of that howse /
10 to be seyn, howħ the fyer commyng to that howse / touchid the pynnycles / leuyng them half brent / but witħ the feitħ of the womman hit was putte a-wey, and lefte them so halfe brent. But ther were neir howsys rigħt nygħ by / the whiche aɫɫ were consumyd and turnyd yn̄-to Asshys. Loo, howħ by the merytis of the
15 blessid Apostle Barthilmewe / the fyer hadde forʒeit the mygħt of his vertu / that the howse shulde nat feiɫɫ his brennyng, that bar his tokyne.

* [f. 77 v.]

GLOSSARY.

Abouyne, *prep.* above, 28/11
Abydde, *ppl.a.* awaited, 15/17 ; *pt.pl.* abyded, 52/22
Accendid, *pt.* 3 *s.* inflamed, 19/5, 47/13
Adherent, *pr.p.* adhering, 9/1
A-downcast, *n.* overthrow, destruction, 5/7 (*not in N.E.D.*). *See also* Downecastyng.
Aduocatte, *n.* patron, 20/24
Affecte, *n.* effect, 37/33
Affluent, *ppl.a.* flowing in abundance, copious, 38/33
Aforyn, *prep.* before, 15/20
Aftir, according to, 47/5
Ageyne, *prep.* against, 2/10
Aggregat, *pt.* 3 *s.* assembled, 1/17
Agnicioun, *n.* acknowledgement, 1/13
Aȝeyne-criynge, *verb n.* repeated crying, 53/11
Allegacion, *n.* assertion, plea, 6/22
Alleggyng, *pr.p.* offering, 18/24
Allightith, *pr.* 3 *s.* makes light, 27/11
Alterid, *pt.pl.* wrangled, 42/8 (*not in N.E.D.*)
A-monge, *av.* from time to time, 40/23, 46/22
Ampliat, *ppl.a.* enlarged, amplified, 35/8
And, if, 26/11, 39/16
Anenst, *prep.* towards, 44/22
Angely, angelic, 32/19
A-noone, anoyn, anon, 23/22, 26/26
Antell, *n.* (*scribal error for* ancell) weights, a balance, 29/14
Anumbrith, *pr.* 3 *s.* numbers, 9/4
Anyhe, *av.* nigh, 22/15
Applied, *pt.* 3 *s.* landed, 62/26
Arayed, *ppl.a.* prepared, 15/25
Areysid, *pt.* 3 *s.* raised, 6/24 ; *pt.* 3 *s.* arysyd, 7/30 ; *ppl.a.* areysid, areysed, 13/35, 17/21
Areysyd, *pt.pl.* arose, 22/20 ; *pt.* 3 *s.* a-roose, 24/15 ; areis, 42/8
Article, moment, 7/9, 16/28, 43/32
Artid, *pt.p.* confined, 37/27 ; *pr.* 3 *s.* artyth, restricts, 39/6
A-sidehalfe, about, 11/2

Askape, *inf.* escape, 43/29 ; *pr.p.* askapynge, 40/14
Aske, *inf.* seek after, 55/36 ; *pr.p.* askyng, proceeding towards, 43/13
Aspyes, *pl.n.* spies, 36/34 ; O.F. espie
Assemblynge, *pr.p.* likening, 13/6
Astonyd, astonyid, *pt.p.* astonished, 13/35, 14/2
Astonyynge, astonishment, 43/5
Attaste, *inf.* try, tempt, 7/31
Attendawntly, *av.* carefully. 48/7
Attendid, *pt.p.* awaited, 49/17
Autoure, *n.* author, 7/10
Avawntynge, *pr.p.* raising, 18/32
Avowe, *n.* vow, 4/22 ; *pl.* avowys, 22/17
Avowe, *inf.* vow, 39/25 ; *pr.* 1 *s.* 41/33 ; *pt.* 3 *s.* avowid, 60/28
Awayte, *n.* ambush, 36/34
Awne, *a.* own, 30/4
Awter, auter, auctur, *n.* altar, 34/5, 38/6, 47/12
Axses, *obs. form of Access, in special sense of Attack,* ague, 51/14

Be, *pt.p.* been, 62/3 ; *pr.pl.* arne, 9/18, bene, 32/8, ar, 33/13, be, 39/2, ben, 8/3, 56/27
Beccence, *a.* of Bec, 34/16
Beeseke, *inf.* beseech, 18/21 ; *pr.pl.* beseke, 32/40 ; *pr.p.* besekynge, 35/18
Befill, *pt.* 3 *s.* befell, 44/28
Begone, *pt.p.* begun, 4/25 ; *ppla.* 45/27
Behestynge, *pr.p.* promising, 8/32 ; *pt.* 3 *s.* behestid, 16/5
Beiste, beyste, *n.* beast, 4/29, 7/27 ; *pl.* beystys, 60/13
Beit, *pt.pl.* beat, 37/15 ; *pr.p.* betynd, 36/10
Beke, *n.* beck, 44/9
Berkyng, *ppl.a.* barking, 15/37
Besekers, beseechers, 35/21
Besy, *a.* busy, 21/16
Besynes, *n.* business, 8/24
Be-taken, betake, *pt.p.* delivered, 46/19, 51/7

Glossary. 65

Bettir to haue, to be better, 59/4
Bidith, *pr.* 3 *s.* expects, 15/31
Bilyng, bylynge, bylyng, *n.* building, 12/28, 13/8, 35/8
Bisy, *adv.* continually, 31/25
Blandysh, blandishment, 46/1
Bleriednes, *n.* bleared condition, 35/25
Bocherie, *n.* community of butchers, 25/30
Bocheyr, *n.* butcher, 25/1 ; *pl.* **bochers**, 25/5
Bollnyng, *ppl.a.* swelling, 29/26
Bore, *pt.p.* borne, 60/6
Boryne, *ppla.* born, 2/26
Bowablenesse, pliability, 28/8
Brede, breid, bread, *heading to Chap.* 7, *p.* 43, 44/18
Breith, breath, 29/11
Brennynge, *pr.p.* burning, 62/7 ; *verb n.* **brennyng**, 63/16 ; *ppl.a.* **brent**, 63/11
Brethen, *n.* brewing, 26/12
Breyste, *n.* breast, 48/4 ; *pl.* **brystys**, 52/24
Brosynge, *verb n. tr. L. contricione*, bruising, 37/23
Browghtyn, *pt.pl.* brought, 15/3
Brystys. *See* **Breyste**.
Byle, *inf.* build, 16/1; *pt.p.* **bylid**, 12/17, **bilid**, 24/20 ; *ppl.a.* **bylyd**, 14/2
By-synne, *tr. L. facinoris*, sin, 36/33

Caase, case, occurrence, chance, plight, 38/21, 54/36
Carpe[n]te, carpent, *n.* litter, 50/22 and 28
Cause, for c., because, 14/28
Cautelys, wiles, 48/11
Celebrite, *n.* solemnity, celebration, 35/14
Cesith, *pr.* 3 *s.* ceases, 34/9 ; *pr.* 2 *s.* **cessist**, 54/30 ; *pt.* 3 *s.* **cesid, cessid**, 39/31, 54/25
Cevefull, *n.* sieve-full, 26/16
Ceves, sieves, 26/10
Chanons, canons, 40/25
Charge, *inf.* regard, 33/12
Chastynge, *verb n.* chastising, 33/4
Chesist, *pr.* 2 *s.* choosest, 14/16
Cheyr', cheir, chere, appearance, countenance, 13/3 and 25, 61/15
Clensyn, *pr.pl.* cleanse, 32/25
Cley, *a.* clay, 33/19
Cleys, *n.* claws, 8/30
Coactid, *pt.p.* compelled, 13/2
Coartid, *pt.p.* constrained, 54/12
Collecte, *n.* collection, 39/29
Compayr, *n.* companion, equal, 24/23
Comyne, comyn, *a.* common, 5/22, 47/15

Comyne, *inf.* have intercourse, 25/15
Conceyuyd, *pt.* 3 *s.* apprehended, knew, 54/15
Conculcacioun, a treading under foot, 32/30
Concytyseyns, fellow-citizens, 22/19
Confortid, *pt.p.* strengthened, 5/38 ; *pt.* 3 *s.* 6/24 ; *ppl.a.* **comforttid**, 13/16 ; *pr.p.* **confortynge**, comforting, 45/12
Consecutyng, *pr.p.* attaining, gaining, 23/12
Constaunce, constancy, 16/4
Constructe, *ppl.a.* constructed, 14/2
Contempne, *inf.* despise, 32/14 ; *pt.pl.* co[n]**tempnyd**, 45/21
Contract, *ppl.a.* crippled, *title of Chap.* 13, *p.* 18 ; *pt.p.* **contracte**, contracted, 27/15
Contray, *n.* country, 4/16, 36/25
Contriciones, *pl.n.* bruises, 23/15
Coshynys, *pl.n.* cushions, 2/29
Cosyn, cousin, 52/7
Cotempned. *See* **Contempne**.
Cowde, could, 37/31
Crucyat, *pt.p.* afflicted, tortured, 37/29
Cryiste, *pr.* 2 *s.* criest, 54/29
Cryistis, crystes, crystys, *gen.s.* 26/6, 33/29, 34/27, 60/9
Crystyne, *a.* Christian, 34/27
Cum, *pr.pl.* come, 39/26 ; *pt.* 3 *s.* **comme**, 39/37 ; *pt.p.* **cummyn**, 16/21, **come**, 39/2 ; *ppl.a.* **cumme**, 40/12
Cumpasse, *inf.* go round, 24/26 ; *pt.* 3 *s.* **cumpasid**, *tr. Lat. cireumferebat*, proclaimed, 13/21
Cumpasse, *n.* course, round, journey, 26/3
Cumplyn, Compline, 24/8
Cunnynge, knowledge, 1/19, 13/17, 34/19
Cure, *n.* care, 10/14 ; spiritual charge or office, 14/23
Curse, *n.* course, 22/1
Cymytory, cemetery, 10/32
Cyteseyne, cityseyn, citizen, 25/27, 39/19 ; *pl.* **cityeens, 39/13

Dampnyd, *pt.p.* condemned, 12/26
Defawtid, *pt.pl.* failed, 21/22
Defawtynge, *verb n.* failing, 45/10
Deformyd, *pt.p.* dishonoured, 15/27
Deif, deaf, 31/27
Deith, death, 38/18
Denay, *inf.* deny, 57/1 ; *pt.* 1 *s.* **denayid**, 44/13 ; *pt.p.* **denayid**, 44/5, **denayd**, 54/23
Departe, *inf.* part, divide, share, 26/9 ; *pr.pl.* **depart**, 55/23 ; *pt.p.* **departid**, separated, 22/30

FOUNDATION F

Depid, *pt.* 3 *s.* dipped, 20/11
Depnesse, *n.* depth, 5/4
Deputid, deputat, *pt.p.* consigned, set, 12/25, 15/18, 44/4, 32/15
Derkenys, darkness, 17/23
Derkid, *pt.p.* darkened, 57/21
Derogacioun, detraction from the honour of, 15/2
Descense, descent, 40/31
Deseit, deceit, 7/13
Deseyuer', deceiver, 14/28
Desirid, *ppl.a.* desired, 22/2
Detrimente, injury, 24/4
Dettefult, *a.* owing, 54/6
Devir, duty, 42/17
Deynrye, *n.* deanery, 47/22
Deyp, *a.* deep, 43/3; *comp.* **depper,** 5/5
Dilaid, *pt.p.* delayed, 29/6
Diserte, *a.* fluent, eloquent, 24/12
Disparyschydde, *pt.* 3 *s.* disappeared, 6/8, **disparisshid,** 19/32, 45/15, **dysperyshid,** 41/5
Dispeyrid, *ppl.a.* despaired of, 23/6
Doer, doyr, door, 37/37, 5/35
Dome, *n.* decree, judgement, 46/17; *pl.* **domys,** 51/9
Dome, *a.* dumb, 31/27
Donward, *av.* downward, 5/2
Doone, *pt.p.* done, 32/12, **doyn,** 9/19, 15/13, 56/27; *ppl.a.* **y-doyne,** 20/20, **y-done,** 31/7
Doughtyng, *pr.p.* doubting, 61/27
Downecastyng, *verb n.* overthrow, destruction, 9/11. *See also* **A-downcast.**
Dowtable, *a.* doubtful, uncertain, 6/11, 43/12
Drawghtis, inclinations, impulses, 48/13
Drayf, *pt.* 3 *s.* drove, 37/23
Dredfult, *a.* full of dread, 48/33
Dressed, *pt.* 3 *s.* addressed, 10/1; *pt.pl.* **dressid them,** went, 22/24
Dropyk, dropik, *a.* dropsical, 29/22 *and heading to Chap.* 29
Drye, *a.* withered, 31/26
Duplynge, *pr.p.* doubling, 63/1
Duryd, *pt.* 3 *s.* lasted, 59/22
Dye, *pr.subj.* 3 *s.* die, 42/3; *pr.pl.* **dyen,** 41/27
Dysesys, diseases, 50/26
Dyvulgate, dywlgate, *pt.p.* spread abroad, 19/5, 25/30

Edifie, *inf.* build, 10/21; *pt.* 3 *s.* **edified,** 31/15
Eere, ere, *n.* ear, 61/21, 42/25; *pl.* **erys,** 35/24, 43/26
Eiste, *a.* East, 10/30
Eiyn, *see* **Yie.**

Elacion, elacyon, vain-glory, pride, elevation, 7/28 and 29
Emynente, *a.* prominent, protruding, high, 12/24
Encres, encresse, encrece, *n.* increase, 1/4, 26/26, 27/18
Endewid, *ppl.a.* endowed, 17/8
Engynnys, *n.* tricks, 49/29
Erryng, *pr.p.* wandering, 46/22
Eschangynge, *verb n.* exchanging, 54/8
Evyn), *a.* equal, 31/7; **euyn crystene,** fellow-Christians, 55/12
Euynly, *av.* in proportion, equally, 35/4
Examinacioun, *n.* Judgement, 12/11
Excitament, *n.* incitement, 31/10
Expert, was —, *pt.* 3 *s.* proved by experience, 28/10; *pr.pl.* **be expert,** prove by experience, 62/13
Expowne, *inf.* expound, 27/10
Eyr', *n.* air, 38/16

Fader, fadyr, father, 1/16, 55/27; *pl.* **fadres,** 34/28
Febelid, *ppl.a.* enfeebled, 23/5
Federyd, *ppl.a.* feathered, 7/21
Felowly, *a.* sociable, 3/10, 34/18
Felowschippe, felschipe, feleshippe, fellowship, 6/24, 37/11, 40/17
Fenny, *a.* swampy, 12/23
Fer', ferre,!far, 21/30, 29/6
Ferid, *pt.* 3 *s.* feared, 63/5
Ferramentis, *pl.* shackles, 37/34
Festfult, *a.* festival, 35/14
Festnyd, *ppl.a.* fastened, 38/24
Filt, fil, fyll, *pt.* 3 *s.* fell, 23/19, 61/24, 62/21, 25/4, 50/2. *See also* **Fyllyn.**
Flawndrys, Flanders, 38/14
Flittynge, *ppl.a.* drifting, 43/24; **flittyng,** vacillating, 6/10, 56/20
Flow, *pt.* 3 *s.* flew, 63/7
Fomynge, *pr.p.* foaming, 50/10
Fonnysch, *a.* rather foolish, 3/16
For, *a.* fore, 39/36
Forgyd, *ppl.a.* forged, 40/3
Forʒeit, *pt.p.* forgotten, 63/15
Former, *n.* Maker, 38/32
Forsayed, forseyed, *ppl.a.* forsaid, 37/26, 62/19
For why, forwhy, because, 3/16, 33/31, 44/15, 47/16
Foryeuennesse, *n.* forgiveness, 39/5
Fote, foit, *n.* foot, 58/10 and 15; *pl.* **feit,** 18/3, **feite,** 58/14
Fowndatoure, foundatoure, *n.* founder, 19/11, 31/9
Fowylle, *a.* foul, 48/35
Fray, *n.* fear, 48/26
Fremyshid, *pt.* 3 *s.* shuddered, 5/8
Fulbreue, *a.* very short, 10/31

Glossary. 67

Fulfiłł, *inf.* fill to the full, 55/14; *pt.* 3 *s.* fulfillid, 49/35; *pt.pl.* fulfillid, 50/7
Fundament, fowndament, *n.* foundation, 2/21, 31/15; *pl.* fowndementys, 18/16
Furowlonges, *pl.* furlongs, 61/21
Fyllyn, *pt.pl.* fell, hastened, 19/8

Gaderynge, gaderyng, *verb n.* gathering, 26/4, 39/29; *pt.p.* gaderyd, 50/7; *ppl.a.* i-gaderid, 4/17
Gallowus, *a.* fit for the gallows, 37/4
Gendrys, *pl.* kinds, 8/4
Gentyly, *a.* Gentile, 14/8
Gestys, *pl.n.* deeds, 11/14
Gete, *pt.p.* got, 55/17
Gobettemele, be —, piecemeal, 22/7
Godly, *av.* divinely, 9/28
Gowyne, *pt.p.* given, 6/17
Grennyng, *pr.p.* grinning, 20/5
Greve, greyf, *n.* grief, 27/18, 29/23, 45/17
Greyce, Greyke, *n.* Greece, *title to Chap.* 9, and 12/5
Gruge, *inf.* grumble, complain, 15/2
Gyf, ȝeue, *inf.* give, 56/11, 41/1, 53/8; *pr.p.* ȝeuyng, 58/20, yeuynge, 60/21; *pt.* 3 *s.* ȝaf, 15/22, ȝaue, 56/20, 61/25, yaue, 62/32; *pt.pl.* ȝaue, 60/18, yeue. 53/12, ȝeif, 40/28; *pt.p.* gowyne, 6/17, ȝeuyn, 40/31, ȝevyne, 54/38, ȝeue, 59/11; *ppl.a.* i-ȝeuen, 38/9, ȝeuyn, 40/32, y-govyn, 53/18, ȝeuen, 55/24

ȝaue, ȝeif, ȝeuyng, etc., *see* Gyf.
ȝeit, *see* ȝitte.
ȝere, year, 34/28; *pl.* ȝerys, 33/18
ȝermoweth, Yarmouth, 27/24
ȝiftes, *see* Yifte.
ȝitte, yet, 4/9; yete, 21/19; ȝit, 31/14; ȝeit, 63/9.
ȝoe, yea, 55/2
ȝyf, if, 41/33

Habowndid, *pt pl.* abounded, 55/31; *pr.p.* habowndynge, 12/23; *ppl.a* 26/25
Haldyng, *pr.p.* holding, 10/26
Halfe, *inf.* halve, 3/20
Halowys, relics or shrines of saints, 32/25, 32/30
Hammys, *pl.* thighs, 58/12
Han, *pr.pl.* have, 31/11
Hastly, *av.* hastily, 19/27, 49/20
Haunttid, *pt.p.* practised or used habitually, frequented, 14/6, 31/18; hawntid, 40/30; *pt.* 3 *s.* hawntid, 2/32; *ppl.a.* hawntid, frequent, 17/11

Hede, *n.* head, 21/9
Hedir, hydyr, hither, 40/32, 43/18
Hedis, *pl.n.* summits, 22/3
Hefker, heifer, 41/22
Heigge, *pr.subj.* 3 *s.* hedge, 33/2
Heip, *n.* heap, 25/28; *pl.* hepys, 43/16
Heir, here, 32/32, 40/29
Here, *inf.* hear, 39/16; *pr.subj.pl.* 39/16
Herte, *gen.s.* heart's, 19/9
He-stunyid, *ppl.a.* astounded, 21/6
Hete, *n.* heat, 28/12
Heuynnes, *pl.n.* heavens, 40/31
Hewerrys, *n.* hewers, 29/16
Hey, *n.* hay, 42/9
Hidde, *inf.* hide, 20/6; *pt.p.* i-hidde, 9/18
Hoist, *n.* sacrifice, 59/8; hoyste, host, 54/1
Hole, *a.* whole, 34/26
Holsumly, *av.* wholesomely, 9/10
Holpyn, *pt.p.* helped, 34/6
Hostrye, *n.* hostelry, 61/7
Howseholde-fadir, father of the household, 21/7
Hyng, *pt.pl.* hung, 18/4

I-callid, *ppl.a.* called, 40/4
I-contracte, *ppl.a.* contracted, 49/2
I-doyne, *ppl.a.* done, 20/20
I-feiłł, *pt.* 3 *s.* befell, 7/22
I-go, *ppl.a.* gone, 26/17
I-know, *ppl.a.* known, 27/6; *pt.p.* y-know, 47/4, knowe, 57/12
I-ȝeuen, *ppl.a.* given, 38/9
I-lette, *ppl.a.* prevented, 55/30
I-losid, *see* Losid.
In-contynent, *av.* forthwith, 13/23
Incrementys, degrees, 29/12
Inflacion), *n.* swelling, 29/26
Infleote, *inf.* bend down, 5/1
Inquerid, *pt.p.* inquired, 7/20
Insignys, *pl.n.* tokens, 33/31
Intendyng yn, attending to, 3/4. *See also* Yntendyng.
Ionys, *gen.s.* John's, 23/4
Ioyest, *pr.* 2 *s.* rejoicest, 55/28; *pr.p.* ioynge, 53/28; *pt.* 3 *s.* ioyed, 35/21; *pt.pl.* ioyid, 35/26; *pt.* 3 *s.* ioyid, enjoyed, 35/25
I-seyne, *ppl.a.* seen, 48/26
I-sublymate, *ppl.a.* honoured, exalted, 17/9
Iubeit, *n.* gibbet, 12/25
Iugys, *pl.* judges, 57/3
Iurye, *n.* Jewry, 7/11

Kechyn), kychyne, *n.* kitchen, 21/2, 28/15

F 2

68   Glossary.

Knowleche, n. acquaintances, 9/21
Knowlegge, n. acknowledgement, 38/6
Knytte, inf. add, 62/19
Kunnynge, kunnyng, n. knowledge, learning, 9/13, 33/9, 15/14
Kyndely, av. readily, 62/10
Kyt, ppl.a. cut, 42/31

Laborynge, ppl.a. struggling, distressed, 51/3
Labur, n. labour, 27/11; pl. labourous, 4/27, laboures, 27/11
Laches, inf. disregard, neglect, 6/19; pr.p. lachesynge, 6/20; pr. 2 pl. lacches. 52/29
Laife, n. laity, 13/19, 19/6
Lake, inf. lack, 25/37
Late, inf. let, 61/8
Laude, n. praise, 11/2
Leche, n. leech, physician, 23/21
Ledde, pt. 3 s. passed, 27/14
Left, ppl.a. lifted, 57/23
Lefully, av. lawfully, 4/15
Leid, pt.p. led, 52/8
Leisse, conj. lest, 13/33
Lemman, n. mistress, 48/1
Lenger' of, farther off, 10/20
Lessynge, verb n. lessening, 25/20
Lettyng, pr.p. preventing, 16/27, 47/7; ppl.a. i-lette, prevented, 55/30
Leue, inf. live, 14/21, 52/22; pr.p. leuyng, 41/22, 45/6; verb. n. leuynge, 3/10
Leuefull, a. lawful, 9/29
Leuer, rather, 26/14
Leyfte, inf. lift, 29/4; pr.p. leftynge, 37/35; pt. 3 s. leift, 43/17; ppl.a. left, 57/23, lyfte, 50/33
Leyid, pt. 3 s. laid, 37/2
Liberttid, pt.p. endowed with liberties or privileges, 16/8
Licencyous, quasi-av. freely, 31/6
Lose, imp.s. loose, 19/28; pr. 3 s. losith, 27/3; pt. 3 s. losid, 57/32; pt.p. losyd, 24/8, losid, 38/20; ppl.a. losid, 18/31, i-losid, 37/35
Loste, lost, n. loss, 19/21, 55/3
Lucur', lucre, 38/11
Lyfte, a. left, 22/28, 35/30
Lykewyse, by a —, in the same way, 34/8
Lyuelode, livelihood, 18/10

Machynamentis, pl. contrivances, 37/36
Malignyng, ppl.a. maligning, 49/36
Malyngnours, n. slanderers, maligners, 16/11
Marchawntis, merchants, 38/10

Maryce, n. marsh, 12/22
Medillid, pt.p. mixed, 14/30; pt. 3 . medyllyd, 46/23
Meide, mede, n. meed, 25/37, 26/24
Meitt, pt.pl. met, 37/4
Mercyable, a. merciful, 55/16
Meritory, meritorie, a. meritorious, 1/1, 34/2
Mersmentis, pl.n. amercements, 37/8
Mete, n. meat, 28/24
Metynge, verb n. measuring, 26/21
Metyrly, av. metrically, 34/21 (Lat. MS. metrice)
Meve, inf. move, 38/3; verb n. mevyng, 31/32; pt. 3 s. mevid, 25/6; pt.p. mewyd, 6/11, mevyd, 25/21, meuyd, 38/14
Meveable, a. movable, 31/24; meveable, changeable, 38/12
Meyn, be m. for, intercede for, 44/2; **by the meyn of,** through the intercession of, 59/14
Mochyll, a. much, 9/14. See also **Mykil.**
Modyr, modir, n. mother, 40/24, 41/7; gen. s. modir-is, 42/30
Monyschid, pt. 1 s. admonished, 53/5
Moo, a. more, 7/15, 20/21
Most, must, 22/4
Moweth, n. mouth, 5/9, 13/32; pl. mowthis, 18/18
Myddis, n. middle, 38/26
Mykil, much, 21/24; **in as mykil,** inasmuch, 33/23; **in so mykill, yn so mykill,** insomuch, 13/10, 52/22. See also **Mochyll.**
Mynnysse, inf. diminish, 9/31; ppl.a. **mynuschyd,** 21/12; pt.p. **mynusid,** 22/7; verb n. **mynyssynge,** 25/20
Mynystris, mynystrys, pl. ministers, 24/26, 26/16, 37/9
Mysterially, av. mystically, 7/24

Nakidly, av. utterly, 40/14
Namely, namly, especially, 2/6, 6/30, 33/30
Nat, not, 4/9, etc.
Nature, of n. (translator's error. Lat. MS., mature, speedily), 38/18
Nedysly, av. necessarily, 22/4
Newydde, ppl.a. renewed, 31/22
Nobiley, n. nobility, 48/40
Noon, pron. none, 21/17
Nothir, nethir, neither, 32/11, 40/29
Nothy (tr. Lat. nothi), a. the Bastard, 10/32
Noye, inf. grieve, trouble, 41/18; verb n. **noyyng,** 48/17
Nul, pr.subj. 1 pl. will not, 39/2

Numbryd, to be —, able to be counted, 27/17 ; *verb n.* numberynge, 26/19 ; *pt.* 3 *s.* numberid, 26/21
Nye, nygħ, nygħe, *a.* nigh, 24/26, 34/5, 47/22, 39/34

Obite, *n.* death, 35/12
Obsequy, *n.* service, 9/31, 40/32
Obuencyouns, obuencyons, *pl.* incidental revenues, 31/22, 34/5
Of, off, 10/20, 42/31 ; fer of, far off, 11/15 ; y-put of, put off, 22/22
Officyne, *n.* office, workshop, recognised place, 14/4
Omysid, *pt.p.* omitted, 33/28, 62/6
On*e*, *prep.* on, by, 24/5, 27/14, 58/12
Ony, *a.* any, 19/25, 26/11
Onyd, *pt.p.* united, 57/21
Onys, *av.* once, 7/4
Oo, one, 39/16 and 19, 60/15
Oon, oone, one, 28/16, 32/4
Oon*e*, *prep.* on, 29/20
Oonly, only, 32/12
Opposid, *pt.p.* examined, questioned, 56/35
Opteyne, *inf.* obtain, 3/8 ; *pt.* 3 *s.* optenyd, 6/23
Opyn*e*, *inf.* open, 62/1 ; *ppl.a.* open, revealed, known, 44/24, 59/10
Or, before, 8/12
Or els . . . or els, either . . . or, 26/7
Othir, othur, othyr, *pron.pl.* others, 18/13, 55/9, 25/6 and 20, 32/3
Othir . . . othir, either . . . or, 18/12
Othys, oaths, 55/12
Ouercummyn, ouercumme, *ppl.a.* overcome, 25/22, 38/29
Ou*er* party, *n.* upper part, surface, 39/37
Ouerplues, *n.* surplus, remnant, 6/31
Ouerwher' (*scribal error for* owher), everywhere, 20/25
Owte-landisshe, *a.* strange, foreign, 4/11
Oynnementys, *pl.* ointments, 31/20

Paase, pase, paysse, *n.* pace, 37/40, 39/36, 51/15
Palle, garment, vestment, 37/5
Pament, pavement, 30/1
Papassie, Papacy, 34/29
Parseueraunte, *ppl.a.* persevering, 13/25
Payse, *n.* weight, 37/38
Pees, *inf.* appease, 55/24 ; *subj.* 3 *s.* peys, 39/15
Peis, *n.* piece, 25/23
Pertynencis, *pl.* appurtenances, appendages, minor properties, 16/7

Pesible, *a.* peaceful, 38/19
Pesibly, *av.* peacefully, 20/2
Peytt, *n.* peal, 37/26
Peysyd, *pt.p.* weighed, considered, 10/10
Pite, *n.* mercy, pity, 61/13
Pituous, *a.* full of mercy, 52/16
Plener*e*, *a.* full, 3/21
Plenytude, fulness, 26/22
Pleys, *pl.* sports, 56/28
Plowe, *n.* plough, 47/2
Porrecte, *inf.* direct, present, offer, extend, 22/11 ; *pr.p.* porrectynge, 18/23 ; *pt.* 3 *s.* porrectid, 44/18
Precedent, *a.* former, 38/31
Prepositure, *n.* provostship, 34/10
Prese, prees, preysse, *n.* crowd, 3/1, 34/23, 46/23
Presente, *pr.pl.* summon, nominate, 55/13
Presydde, *pt.pl.* pressed, 31/30
Pretende, *pr.pl.* set forth, show, present, 7/12 ; *pr.p.* pretendynge, 5/10 ; *pt.* 3 *s.* pretendid, 12/21, 13/2 ; *pt.pl.* pretendid, presaged, 38/18
Preuent, *inf.* outdo, 25/33
Preuydyd, *pt.* 3 *s.* provided, 2/14
Priuatid, *pt.p.* deprived, 45/5, priuate, 46/5
Producte, *ppl.a.* produced, derived, 14/10
Proferred, *pt.* 3 *s.* put forth, presented, 13/23 ; *pt.p.* proferid, brought forth, produced, 42/20
Proficye, *n.* prophecy, 32/7
Promouyd, *pt.* 3 *s.* promoted, 34/16
Prompte, *a.* ready, 31/17 ; in prompte, in readiness, 34/20
Promytte, *pr.* 1 *s.* promise, 25/18
Propre, propyr', *a.* own, 41/12, 9/30
Prostratte, *pt.* 3 *s.* prostrated, 27/25
Prowte, *a.* proud, 6/20
Pryse, *n.* price, 42/4

Quantite, quantyte, *n.* mass, size, 18/6, 22/25
Querett, quarett, *n.* complaint, plea, cause, 15/26, 16/24
Qwyke, *a.* living, 32/32, 40/21

Range, *pt.* 3 *s.* rang, 27/27 ; *pt.p.* roonge, 37/26
Rathir', *av.* sooner, 3/8
Raueyn, *n.* robbery, 55/22
Recreacioun, *n.* refreshment, comfort, 4/16
Recreate, *pt.* 3 *s.* refreshed, 45/27
Reducyng, *pr.p.* recalling, 3/30 ; *pt.* 3 *s.* reducid, brought back, 35/13

Glossary.

Remembrith, *pr.* 3 *s.* records, mentions, 8/13; **rememberid,** *ppl.a.* already mentioned, 31/14
Rennyth, *pr.* 3 *s.* runs, 31/4; *pr.p.* **rennynge,** 23/24, 37/11
Renvydde, *pt.pl.* renewed, 31/20
Reparacioun, *n.* restoration, 35/23
Repercioun (*scribal error for* re[cu]percioun, *tr.* Lat recuperacione), *n.* recovery, *heading to Chap.* 27, *p.* 61.
Reprevid, *pt.* 3 *s.* reproved, 37/6
Resunne, resone, *n.* reason, 31/5, 33/13
Returnyd, *ppl.a.* bent or turned back, 26/29, 35/32; *pt.pl.* 18/5
Reysith, *pr.* 3 *s.* raises, 27/4
Roys, roos, rooys, *pt.* 3 *s.* rose, 27/30, 37/1, 59/7
Rycchynge, *verb n.* enriching, 55/8; *ppl.a.* **rychessid,** enriched, 17/10
Ryvelyd, *a.* wrinkled, furrowed, 27/16

Sadde, *a.* serious, mature, 24/18; *comp.* **sadder,** *a.* more serious, more mature, 38/27
Saf, Salfe, *a.* safe, 21/11, 53/9
Sam, *a.* same, 16/7
Sauacyoun, *n.* salvation, 21/18
Sayed, seied, *ppl.a.* said, 27/13, 41/24
Sayynge, *pr.p.* essaying, trying, 51/15
Scapis, *pl.* transgressions, 3/30
Scapynge, *verb n.* escaping, 22/9; *pr.p.* **skapyng,** 38/4, **askapynge,** 40/14; *pt.* 3 *s.* **skapid,** 49/29; *pt.p.* **skapid,** 15/24
Schete, *inf.* shut, 20/5
Schoone, *pt.* 3 *s.* shone, 15/34
Scochyn, *n.* escutcheon, 17/3
Secrete, *av.* secretly, 15/19 (*tr.* Lat. inauditum. *Not in N.E.D. as av.*)
Seke, *inf.* seek, 24/27; *pr.pl.* 33/29
Seker', *n.* seeker, 5/30
Sekyr, sekir, *a.* sure, 2/13, 14/3
Senowys, synowys, *pl.* sinews, 27/15, 28/7 and 23
Sentence, *n.* opinion, way of thinking, judgement, significance, 6/11; *pl.* 6/22, 7/13
Seryous, *a.* arranged in sequence, 7/3; *cp.* med. Lat. seriose, *adv.* (*not in N.E.D.*)
Sesid, *pt.* 3 *s.* ceased, 43/27; *pt.p.* **i-sesid,** 44/10
Sesyne, *inf.* apprehend, arrest, 57/2
Sey, sye, *pt.pl.* saw, 2/22, 22/22, 61/7; *pt.* 1 *s.* **sawhe,** 8/14; *pt.* 3 *s.* **sawe, sawh,** 23/27, 38/1; *pt.p.* **seyne, seyn,** 17/6, 18/33, 20/22; *verb n.* **seyng,** 36/18; *ppl.a,* **i-seyne,** 48/26

Sey, seye, *inf.* to say, 5/13, 12/15; *pr.p.* **seyynge, seiyng,** 12/16, 40/24; *imp.s.* **sey,** 19/21; *pt.* 1 *s.* **seied,** 8/15; *pt.* 3 *s.* **seyid, seyed,** 19/20, 41/4; *pt.p.* **seied,** 31/4, **seide,** 32/8, **seyed,** 8/14; *ppl.a.* **sayed, seied,** 27/13, 41/24
Seyr, *a.* sere, withered, 28/13
Sheippe, *n.* sheep, 34/3
Shereve, *n.* sheriff, 37/9
Sholde, shold, *pt.pl.* should, 1/2, 32/1 and 28; *pt.* 2 *s.* **shuldes,** 5/14
Shuldrid, *pt.pl.* jostled, pushed with the shoulder, 31/31
Sith, syth, sithen, *conj.* since, 18/8, 62/17, 9/12; **sith,** when, 29/3
Sittynge, sittyng, *ppl.a.* befitting, 25/31, 48/40
Sixtene, *a.* sixteenth, 58/22
Skapyng. *see* **Scapyng.**
Skunfitid, *ppl.a.* vanquished, 56/11
Sloweth, *n.* sloth, 41/14
Slummrynge, *verb n.* slumbering, 61/16
Smothid, *pt.p.* soothed, 46/2
Smyt, *ppl.a.* smitten, 38/24
Sodayne, sodayn, sodeyne, *a.* sudden, 41/16, 52/21, 54/36
Sodenly, sodaynly, *av.* suddenly, 21/3, 37/39
Solempne, *n.* solemnity, 32/5
Son, sonne, *n.* sun, 35/13, 38/15, 61/5
Sondirly, *a.* separate, 16/31
Sondirly, *av.* separately, 16/31
Soper, supper, 33/4
Sownyd, *pt.* 3 *s.* resounded, 24/16; *pt.pl.* sounded, 44/12
Sowyl, soul, 39/16
Sporys, *pl.* spurs, 19/28
Sprongyng, y-sprongyne, *ppl.a.* sprung, 2/26, 12/5
Squarerys, *pl.n.* squarers, 29/17
Squorgyng, *verb n.* scourging, 41/28
Stappys, *pl.n.* steps, 45/14
Stedfastid, *pt.* 3 *s.* made steadfast, 6/25
Sterid, *pt.p.* stirred, 9/24; *pt.* 3 *s.* 13/21; *verb n.* **sterynge,** 25/22
Stoid, *pt.* 3 *s.* stood, 45/12; *pt.pl.*, 11/24, 38/8
Stokkid, *ppl.a.* imprisoned, set in the stocks, 27/4
Stolys, *pl.n.* stools, 18/5
Stonde, *inf.* stand, 26/30; *imp.s.* 50/29; *pr.p.* **stondynge, stondyng,** being at hand, 7/9, 42/19; *verb n.* stepping, 36/16; *pr.* 3 *s.* **stondith yn,** approaches, 39/1. *See also* **Stoid.**
Stonyid, *pt.p.* stupefied, dazed, 43/20
Stonyynge, *verb n.* stupefaction, amazement, 50/9
Stoyne, *n.* stone, 22/4

Glossary. 71

Strange, *a.* strong, 53/30
Streghthyd, *scribal error for* **Strenghthyd**, *ppl.a.* strengthened, 49/3; *pt.p.* **streyngethyd**, 16/19
Streym, *n.* stream, 39/37
Streyt, *a.* strict, stern, 25/2; *comp.* **streyter**, more rigorous, 51/26
Strompethode, *n.* harlotry, 55/26
Suatperynge, *scribal error for* **suatterynge** (Lat. initantem *being taken as* innatantem), *ppl.a.* splashing, fluttering, 6/25
Succurrid, *pt.p.* succoured, 12/11
Sugget, **subiett**, *a.* subject, 57/17, 2/13
Surly, *av.* surely, 37/20
Swage, *inf.* assuage, 25/16; *pt.p.* **swagid**, 35/27
Sweitis, *pl.n.* sweats, 27/11
Swolle, *ppl.a.* swollen, 20/4
Swyfterly, *av.* more swiftly, 45/27
Syke, *a.* sick, 23/25
Syknes, **sykenes**, **siknes**, *n.* sickness, 36/6, 29/1 and 23
Sylle, *inf.* sell, 47/3
Symulate, *ppl.a.* feigned, 15/6

Tabylwyse, *av.* in manner or form of a table. ? In a rectangular shape [N.E.D.], 10/19. (Lat. MS. decenti lapideo tabulatu, with a comely pavement.)
Take, *pt.p.* taken, 25/31, 32/29
Telle, *inf.* count, 26/20
Terys, *pl.n.* tears, 22/32
Than, **thanne**, *av.* then, 5/18, 10/26
That, *rel. pron.* what, 6/9, 23/11
The, *pron.* thee, 5/16, 19/23
Thedir, **thidir**, *av.* thither, 39/27, 54/2
Theifte, *n.* theft, 37/8
Theyfly, *av.* thievishly, 54/16
This, **thyes**, *pl.a.* these, 38/33, 60/19, 3/32
Tho, *a.* those, 44/22
Threid, *n.* thread, 63/3
Thryssheholde, *n.* threshold, 41/23
Thrywh, *pt.* 3 *s.* threw, 46/21
Thyy, *n.* thigh, 28/5; *pl.* **thyis**, **thyys**, **thyes**, 18/4, 26/30, 28/21
Tochith, *pr.* 3 *s.* touches, concerns, 33/28; *pr.p.* **tochynge**, 34/27
Togidir, together, 39/31
Toone, the one, 58/16, 59/21
Tree, *n.* mast, 43/25
Tremelyd, *pt.* 3 *s.* trembled, 5/8; *ppl.a.* **tremulynge**, 52/26
Trewith, *n.* truth, 39/7
Trowblys, *a.* troubled, 53/14
Tutur, **tutoure**, *n.* protector, keeper, 16/6, 21/18

Vnccioun, *n.* unction, 6/28
Vndefawtyng, *ppl.a.* unfailing, 45/8
Vndircrept, *pt.p.* crept under, 40/28
Vndirnym, *inf.* rebuke, 41/1; *pt.* 3 *s.* **vndir-nymdid**, 37/6; *pt.p.* **vndirnymyd**, 25/35
Vndredfully, *av.* without fear, 55/8
Vnexpert, *a.* destitute, 62/31
Vnhabilnesse, *n.* folly, 4/4
Vnkende, *a.* ungrateful, 45/15
Vnlefully, *av.* unlawfully, 48/1
Vnmevable, *a.* immovable, 22/29
Vnneith, *av.* scarcely, 28/24, 39/30
Vnrepreuyd, *ppl.a.* unblameable, irreproveable, 13/27. (Lat. MS. irreprehensibil*is*.)
Vnsessyngly, *av.* unceasingly, 62/4
Vnsittynge, *ppl.a.* unbefitting, 32/35
Vnskunfitid, *ppl.a.* unconquered, invincible, 23/9, 34/30
Vnwarnes, *n.* carelessness, 62/21
Vnwarys, *av.* unawares, 44/34
Vnwastid, *ppl.a.* unexhausted, 61/13
Vnwount, *a.* unusual, 46/4
Vnyd, *pt.p.* united, 14/22
Vplond, in the country, 20/17
Vtas, *n.* octave, 60/1; AF. utaves, OF. oitauves
Vttir, *a.* outer, 29/24
Vttir, *inf.* utter, 34/21
Vengynge, *pr.p.* taking vengeance, 9/5
Ventilatte, *inf.* agitate, 8/16
Ventriclis, ventricles, cavities in the brain, 47/6
Vertu, *n.* might, 21/25; *pl.* **vertues**, deeds of power, 26/27
Voyde, *a.* empty, empty-handed, 25/9, 26/15; **voyde from**, without, 55/36; **voyde**, useless, 49/18
Vylyfycat, *ppl.a.* vilified, 48/24

Walowid, *pt.* 3 *s.* rolled, 30/1; *pr.p.* **wallowynge**, 50/4
Wan, *pt.* 3 *s.* won, 54/4
Wardyng, *pr.p.* guarding, 49/28
Wawys, *pl.n.* waves, 21/33
Waytys, *pl.n.* ambushes, 49/29
Wedir, *n.* weather, 44/30
Wel, *inf.* flow, 18/29
Welsumme, **weylsum**, *a.* fortunate, 6/26, 53/20
Wenyd, *pt.p.* weaned, 42/26
Werith, *pr.* 3 *s.* wears out, 47/8
Werke, *n.* work, 18/17
Wexynge, *pr.p.* waxing, 45/3; *pt.* 3 *s.* **wexid**, **wexed**, 50/36, 52/6
Weyr, *pt.* 3 *s.* wore, 61/15
Wham, *pron.* whom, 5/9
Whan, **whane**, when, 4/27, 23/11, 48/10, 39/26

72 Glossary.

Whidir, whydir, whedyr, whither, 39/26, 3/28, 46/8
Whoes, whois, whoeys, *pron.* whose, 10/8, 19/21, etc.
Wil we . . . **nul we,** willingly or unwillingly, 39/2
Wode, *n.* wood, 29/16; *pl.* **wodis,** woods, forests, 46/22
Wodnesse, wooddenes, wodnes, wodenys, woodnes, *n.* madness, rage, 15/8, 21/3, 38/21, 49/7, 55/20; *gen. s.* **woodnys,** 57/27
Woide, woyde, *a.* mad, furious, 50/36, 45/3
Wolle, *pr.* 3 *s.* is willing, 26/28; *pr.* 2 *s.* **wolt,** 55/35; *pt. subj.* 3 *s.* **wolde,** 51/2, 56/40
Wonde, *n.* wound, 42/34
Wondir, *a.* wondrous, 30/2
Wonte, wounte, woonnte, *a.* usual, wont, 32/2, 39/36, 40/30, 51/2; were **wownte,** 19/24; was **woonte,** 25/3
Worttys, *pl.n.* plants, herbs, 8/11
Wowers, *pl.n.* wooers, 48/10
Wrake, wracke, *n.* destruction, 40/14, 49/15
Wynnyng, *verb n.* gain, profit, 49/14
Wysshe, *pt.* 3 *s.* washed, 20/11
Wytty, *a.* wise, 10/11

Y-callid, *ppl.a.* called, 22/1
Y-caste, *ppl.a.* cast, 43/23
Y-consecrate, *ppl.a.* consecrated, 40/10
Ydle, yn, in vain, 39/33
Y-doyne, *ppl.a.* done, 20/20
Yeldynge, yeldyng, ʒyldynge, *pr.p.* yielding, 27/31, 38/7, 51/22
Yete, Yette, *see* **ʒitte.**

Yeue, ʒeue, *inf.* give, 4/5, 33/7; *imp.* 2 *s.* **yeue,** 6/2; *pr.* 2 *s.* **yeuest,** 25/19; *pr.p.* **yeuynge,** 10/12, ʒeuynge, 35/27; *pt.* 3 *s.* ʒaf, ʒaue, yaue, 15/22, 16/11, 26/16; *pt.pl.* yēue, 53/12; *pt.p.* **gowyne,** 6/17, yeue, 13/29, 19/3, 23/26, ʒeuen, 32/2, ʒeue, 34/25; *ppl.a.* i-ʒeuen, 38/9, y-govyn, 53/18
Yeuer, ʒeuer, *n.* giver, 25/14 and 36
Y-freid, *ppl.a.* freed, 16/9
Y-govyn, *see under* **Yeue.**
Yie, ye, *n.* eye, 5/2, 10/10, heading to Chap. 13. p. 51; *pl.* **yene, eiyn, yis, yen,** 5/28, 8/13, 11/17, 13/10
Yifte, *n.* gift, 27/2, 28/15; *pl.* **yeiftis, ʒiftes,** 25/14, 31/23
Y-knowen, *ppl.a.* known, 3/10; *pt.p.* y-know, 47/4
Y-maade, *ppl.a.* made, 4/23
Ympne, *n.* hymn, 36/11; *pl.* **ympnys,** 37/28
Yncourse, *n.* attack, assault, 8/24
Yndurat, *ppl.a.* hardened, stubborn, 25/12
Ynfoldeyn, *inf.* envelop, enclose, 8/1
Ynfowndid, *pt.p.* infused, 28/12
Y-nowh, enough, 55/38
Ynpridid, *ppl.a.* made proud, 2/9
Ynsawt, *inf.* insult, 25/4
Yntendyng one, listening or attending to, 5/28
Y-nurysshed, *ppl.a.* reared, 24/2
Yough, yougth, *n.* youth, 3/11 and 31
Y-put of, *ppl.a.* put off, 22/22
Y-rotyd, *ppl.a.* rooted, 34/9
Y-schewid, *ppl.a.* shown, 9/28
Y-sped, *ppl.a.* brought to an end, 55/33
Y-streyned, *pt.p.* bound fast, confined, 57/26

The manufacturer's authorised representative in the EU for product safety is Oxford University Press España S.A. of El Parque Empresarial San Fernando de Henares, Avenida de Castilla, 2 - 28830 Madrid (www.oup.es/en or product.safety@oup.com). OUP España S.A. also acts as importer into Spain of products made by the manufacturer.
Printed and bound by CPI Group (UK) Ltd, Croydon, CR0 4YY

20/03/2026

02075329-0006